Language, Literature, and the Negotiation of Identity

UNC | COLLEGE OF ARTS AND SCIENCES
Germanic and Slavic Languages and Literatures

From 1949 to 2004, UNC Press and the UNC Department of Germanic & Slavic Languages and Literatures published the UNC Studies in the Germanic Languages and Literatures series. Monographs, anthologies, and critical editions in the series covered an array of topics including medieval and modern literature, theater, linguistics, philology, onomastics, and the history of ideas. Through the generous support of the National Endowment for the Humanities and the Andrew W. Mellon Foundation, books in the series have been reissued in new paperback and open access digital editions. For a complete list of books visit www.uncpress.org.

Language, Literature, and the Negotiation of Identity
Foreign Worker German in the Federal Republic of Germany

BARBARA A. FENNELL

UNC Studies in the Germanic Languages and Literatures
Number 119

Copyright © 1998

This work is licensed under a Creative Commons CC BY-NC-ND license. To view a copy of the license, visit http://creativecommons.org/licenses.

Suggested citation: Fennell, Barbara A. *Language, Literature, and the Negotiation of Identity: Foreign Worker German in the Federal Republic of Germany.* Chapel Hill: University of North Carolina Press, 1998.
DOI: https://doi.org/10.5149/9781469656526_Fennell

Library of Congress Cataloging-in-Publication Data
Names: Fennell, Barbara A.
Title: Language, literature, and the negotiation of identity : Foreign worker German in the Federal Republic of Germany / by Barbara A. Fennell.
Other titles: University of North Carolina Studies in the Germanic Languages and Literatures ; no. 119.
Description: Chapel Hill : University of North Carolina Press, [1998] Series: University of North Carolina Studies in the Germanic Languages and Literatures. | Includes bibliographical references.
Identifiers: LCCN 97009887 | ISBN 978-1-4696-5651-9 (pbk: alk. paper) | ISBN 978-1-4696-5652-6 (ebook)
Subjects: Foreign workers — Germany (West) — Language. | German language — Study and teaching — Foreign speakers. | Pidgin German. | German language — Social aspects. | Immigrants' writings, German — Germany (West) — History and criticism. | Germany — Emigration and immigration — History — 20th century.
Classification: LCC PF5997 .A4 F46 1997 | DCC 437/ .086/91

For
Stefan and Charlotte

Contents

Preface	xi
Acknowledgments	xiii
Introduction	1
1. Guests and Immigrants: The Historical and Political Background	12
Introduction	12
Foreign Labor from 1864 to the Present: A Historical Overview	13
Conclusion	34
2. The Social Background	35
Introduction	35
Living Conditions	36
Household Structure and Income	38
Education	39
Employment Opportunities	42
Ausländerfeindlichkeit	45
Conclusion	50
3. From *Pidgindeutsch* to Standard German: The Linguistic Situation	51
Introduction	51
Structural Features of Foreign Worker German	52
Varieties of Foreign Worker German	58
Is *Pidgindeutsch* a Pidgin?	64
Overlapping Systems: Pidgins, Creoles, Interlanguages, and Xenolects	69
Recent Changes in *Gastarbeiterlinguistik*	84

> Intended Meaning and Prepositional Usage 86
>
> *Gastarbeiterdeutsch* and the Determination of Ethnic Identity 90

4. Language, Literature, and the Negotiation of Identity 94

> Introduction 94
>
> A Brief History of Literary Activity in the Immigrant Community 95
>
> Common Themes of Immigrant Literature 101
>
> Negotiating Labels 105
>
> The Role of Language in the Negotiation of Ethnic and Social Identity 108
>
> The Developmental Nature of Foreign Worker Literature 124
>
> Literature as Capital: National and Intellectual Forces in the Negotiation of Identity 132

Notes 139

Bibliography 153

Index 165

Preface

It is very difficult as a British subject to write a book which in any way criticizes other countries' treatment of foreigners. I hope that my German colleagues will appreciate that many similar critical works could be (and indeed have been) written about foreigners in Britain and all of the other countries of the European Union. I hope also that they will acknowledge that I have tried to be constructive and positive in my criticism and have attempted to steer clear of polemic and exaggeration in my descriptive accounts.

I am indebted to a number of people who have read part or all of the manuscript and given me helpful comments, in particular to Stefan Pugh, Ian Press, Mark Louden, and two anonymous readers. Thanks are also due to Will Moore, my copyeditor at the University of North Carolina Press. All errors and omissions remaining in the text are of course my sole responsibility. Mike Reynolds and Joan Stewart deserve particular thanks for all their support and encouragement during my years in North Carolina. I miss their companionship and their example. Finally, I would like to thank Paul Roberge for having the faith and patience to coax me through to the end of this project.

Part of the research for this book was funded by a Fellowship of the American Council of Learned Societies 1992–93, whose grant was matched by the College of Humanities at North Carolina State University. I should like to thank both bodies for their generous support of my work.

To my husband Stefan and daughter Charlotte I owe a special debt of gratitude.

Acknowledgments

I would like to acknowledge all of the following for their assistance:

The University of Alabama Press for permission to reprint an emended version of B. A. Fennell, "Literary Data and Linguistic Analysis: The Example of Modern German Immigrant Worker Literature," in *The Text and Beyond: Essays in Literary Linguistics*, edited by Cynthia G. Bernstein (Tuscaloosa: University of Alabama Press, 1994), 241–62.

Language Quarterly for permission to reprint an emended version of B. A. Fennell, "Markers of Ethnic Identity in Immigrant Worker German," *Language Quarterly* 30 (Winter–Spring 1992): 1–19.

Dagyeli Verlag, Frankfurt am Main, for permission to excerpt Levent Aktoprak's *Unterm Arm die Odysee*.

The authors for permission to reprint the following extracts from *In zwei Sprachen Leben*, edited by Irmgard Ackermann (1984): Chantal Estran-Goecke: "Aphasie"; Ivan Tapia Bravo: "Das bin ich mir schuldig"; Franco Biondi: "Sprachfelder" and "Nicht nur gastarbeiterdeutsch."

Deutscher Taschenbuch Verlag (dtv), Munich, for permission to reprint extracts from Rafik Schami's *Die Sehnsucht fährt schwarz* (1988).

Kiepenheuer and Witsch, Cologne, for permission to reprint the extract from page 87 of Günter Wallraff's *Ganz unten* (1985).

Centaurus-Verlagsgesellschaft, Pfaffenweiler, for permission to reprint the poem from Sadi Üçüncü, *Integrationshemmender Faktor: Ausländerfeindlichkeit in der Bundesrepublik Deutschland: ein Überblick zur Theorie der Ausländerfeindlichkeit* (1984).

Franco Biondi, for permission to reprint the extract from *Das Unsichtbare sagen!: Prosa und Lyrik aus dem Alltag des Gastarbeiters*, edited by Habib Bektas (1980).

Deutscher Taschenbuch Verlag (dtv), Munich, for permission to cite from Hülya Özkan in *Eine Fremde wie ich: Berichte, Erzählungen, Gedichte von Ausländerinnen*, edited by Hülya Özkan and Andrea Wörle (1985).

Klartext-Verlag, Essen, for permission to reprint the poem from Pasquale Marino in *Dies ist nicht die Welt, die wir suchen: Ausländer in Deutschland*, edited by Suleman Taufiq (1983).

A1 Informationen Gesellschaft, Munich, for permission to print the extracts from Adel Karasholi's *Wenn Damaskus nicht wäre: Gedichte* (1992).

Das Arabische Buch, Berlin, for permission to reprint part of José F. A. Oliver's poem "im gerippe eines tages."

Language, Literature, and
the Negotiation of Identity

Introduction

Since reconstruction after World War II the German government has repeatedly insisted that Germany is *kein Einwanderungsland* ("not an immigration country"). Yet today there are approaching 7 million foreigners resident in that country, many of whom have lived there for over two decades, and a number of whom represent the third generation of immigrants in their family.

The status of the diverse residents of the Federal Republic is by no means clear-cut, and it has been a controversial topic for a number of years. There are various categories of foreign resident in Germany, as in any European country. Some are students; others are seasonal workers or temporary employees of foreign companies (for example, American and Japanese citizens working in Germany); others are refugees; some are asylum seekers; still others fall into such categories as "foreign spouse of German citizen" or "independent immigrant" under the European Community agreement on freedom of movement and occupation. Furthermore, there are also immigrants of German descent who automatically receive German citizenship on arrival in Germany and are not counted amongst the foreign population at all. The following quotation from Grosch encapsulates the confusion about immigrants' status very neatly, while providing insight into the major groupings:

> Indeed, the word "foreign" has a number of different connotations. There are "indigenous foreigners" as opposed to "alien foreigners," there are Germans with a foreign passport and foreigners with a German passport, there are foreigners from European Community countries and those from outside the EC—a confusing picture for many Germans themselves.
>
> As confusing as this picture is the public debate in which the three groups in question are constantly mixed up. Of the three groups, only two—legally speaking—are foreigners, meaning persons with foreign citizenship. They are:
>
> 1. Foreigners who were called into the country—the majority of foreign workers and their families, the so-called "guest workers."
>
> 2. Those foreigners who came and are still coming to ask for political asylum, a right given to them by the country's constitution.
>
> (1992:134)

Since reunification, foreigners of the second category, refugees and asylum seekers, have become the focus of German unrest and the cause of changes in immigration policy, as they have in other countries of Western Europe; for this reason we will have cause to discuss them further in Chapter 1, when we consider recent developments.

However, this book deals primarily, though by no means exclusively, with foreigners of the first category, that is, those people who were recruited to work in the booming German industry from 1955 onward, many of whom, whether by choice or by default, have stayed in Germany for years or even decades. In German the politically relatively neutral term *Arbeitsmigranten* is used for this group, but there is no direct equivalent in English, where the term "migrant worker" usually connotes, at least in the United States, agricultural workers who move through North America with the crops. By "Arbeitsmigranten" we primarily mean those workers who have migrated since World War II to secure industrial positions, particularly those who have migrated from Mediterranean countries to the industrial areas of Germany.

The problem of what to call the focal group of the present study is exacerbated when we consider the issue of their residential status in Germany. Are persons who have migrated to a country and have lived and worked there for more than twenty years merely "foreign workers," or are they de facto "immigrants," regardless of their legal status even if they still cherish the myth of one day returning to their home country?[1] And can one really call these people "immigrant workers" in the face of the official, government claim that Germany is not an immigration country? Alternatively, can we naively use the German euphemism *Gastarbeiter*, "guest worker," given that it reinforces the one-sided and temporary nature of the workers' position in Germany and that it is considered downright offensive by a number of individuals to whom the term has been applied? The choice is clearly a political one. For this reason, we will maintain the more neutral, English term "foreign worker" as far as possible, using the other terms only when we feel they are justified by the context of the discussion.

In this study, we examine the linguistic, social, psychological, and literary consequences of foreign workers having been conceived of as temporary members of German society. We assess the effects of both the lack of a conscious integration policy by the German government and the perpetual desire of many of the immigrants themselves to return home some day. These developments have obviously had radical effects on the individual and collective identities of foreign workers and their children—effects which we need to explore in detail and from a number of points of view.

For example, like many other minority groups throughout the world, foreign workers in Germany are frequently marked socially by the language they use. *Gastarbeiterdeutsch*, "Guest Worker German," or, using the term I prefer, "Foreign Worker German," results directly from a lack both of formal instruction in the standard language and of opportunity to socialize with native speakers. More highly stigmatized than other German varieties, regional or social, Foreign Worker German creates a dilemma for its users that reinforces the interplay between language use and the expression of personal, group, and ethnic identity. Second-generation immigrants have frequently been said to speak neither the "home language" of their parents nor the "host language" sufficiently well to feel they belong to one group or the other, and they may be branded as "semilingual"—all of which may lead to an identity crisis of crippling proportions, as attested by the alarming school drop-out and worker unemployment rates among foreign workers that only now are beginning to ease (see Chapter 2). However, we must be careful from the outset to distinguish between native-like mastery of the basic structures of language (phonology, morphology, and syntax) and sociolinguistic/pragmatic facility in the standard, educated, middle-class dialect, which is hardly the province of most mainstream Germans in the first place. These issues will be discussed further in Chapter 3.

It would be naive to pretend that language is the root of all the immigrants' problems, of course, and we will need to undertake, in chapters 1 and 2, a detailed examination of the political, social, and economic history that has led to the current situation. Yet it cannot be denied that linguistic difficulties have gone hand in hand with social disruption throughout history, as evinced by the current native-language crisis in the countries of the former Soviet Union and by the persistent African American Vernacular English controversy in the United States. What is crucial here is to attempt to discuss the issues without prejudging them, to be wary of reinforcing nonscientific stereotypes on the one hand and of indulging in *Kopftuchsolidarität* ("head-scarf solidarity") on the other.

This book has several important aims. First, it seeks to bring the work of a large group of German scholars to a wider audience in the literary and linguistic communities. *Gastarbeiterlinguistik* has developed into a recognized subfield of linguistics in Germany and has been an important testing ground for theories of language acquisition, pidgin and creole studies, discourse analysis, multicultural communication, and the sociology of language, to mention but a few. A number of major German research universities (for example, Heidelberg, Free University-Berlin, Wuppertal, Stuttgart, and Konstanz) have research and teaching programs devoted to the Foreign Worker German-speaking sector of the community, and they have made important contributions to the field. For example, they have refined our understanding of critical linguistic concepts, such as pidgin, creole, and learner dialect. They have also produced a significant body of empirical work on the subject of natural second-language acquisition *(ungesteuerter Zweitsprachenerwerb)*, bringing the focus of language-learning studies out of artificial classroom settings and into natural, undirected settings. They have studied the effects of imperfect bilingualism on second-generation immigrants and have made suggestions for the incorporation of multicultural methods into the classroom. More recent work has made contributions in the field of cross-cultural linguistics and interpretive sociolinguistics. This book presents an overview of this important work, albeit a necessarily very selective one.

Second, this book aims to introduce its audience to the rich body of creative work produced by foreigners in Germany that has until recently been largely unheralded in literary circles. This situation has changed in the past ten years, partly thanks to the efforts of the Institut für Deutsch als Fremdsprache in Munich, which has faithfully promoted immigrant literature and, in collaboration with the Bavarian Academy of Fine Arts, has introduced the Adalbert von Chamisso Prize for a work from an author writing in German who does not speak German as a native language. The present work attempts to broaden the audience base for this literature and provide a brief introduction to it for English-speaking scholars of literature and comparative literature. With the strong emphasis of current scholarship on issues of identity and on cultural criticism and cultural studies in general, it seems crucial for scholars to entertain the work of immigrants in Germany, which has identity as its central theme. The whole area of German-immigrant literature has, in fact, received relatively little critical attention hitherto; where it has received attention, commentaries have most often been written by the immigrant writers themselves. In any case, almost all critical work has been written in German. A significant aim of this study, therefore, is to disseminate among a wider audience, a knowledge of this literature, which is richly endowed with cultural, social, ethnic, and historical wisdom.

Germany provides a perfect venue for examining the problems of language and identity. No other country ever gave stronger voice to the principle of "one nation, one language." Indeed, it is from the work of Herder and Fichte that this philosophy develops, and it is a direct result of the influence of these German intellectuals that the general European tradition developed that placed monolingualism at the core of the nation-state. Germany's recent history and its central position in

Europe make it an important laboratory for cross-cultural interaction, and studying it as a special case will enrich our understanding of the problems of intercultural contact and immigration. Indeed, given current reports of *Ausländerfeindlichkeit* ("xenophobia"/"antiforeigner sentiment") in Germany, this book might profitably be read by sociologists as well as a more general public who wish for an understanding of the problems Germany faces today.

My approach to the problems of immigration and identity is fundamentally linguistic. Multilingualism, language contact, and language barriers are central concerns arising inevitably from the sudden juxtaposition of different peoples caused by immigration (Hinnenkamp 1990:279). Indeed, at the heart of most literary and social interpretations of the identity issue in international perspective are exactly such questions as who has a voice and who is silenced by intercultural contact. Direct insight into the linguistic processes and linguistic behavior underlying the transmission of identity is surely central to an understanding of identity issues.

We begin in Chapter 1 with a close examination of the political, economic, and social history of immigration to Germany since the turn of the century. In order to interpret the events of the postwar years, it is essential to consider the constellation of major and minor historical events that have led to the current social and linguistic situation and have dictated current immigration policy. From the outset it is apparent that there is not a single, homogeneous group of foreign workers in Germany, but rather that there is, and always has been, a variety of different types of foreigners, who have arrived in Germany at different times, from different places, and for different reasons. Foreigners in Germany, even foreign workers, have many different faces, which are not constant, but change over time and adapt to different circumstances both in Germany and abroad. Legislation has striven to recognize this variation and keep pace with its changes.

Chapter 2 focuses on some of the central characteristics of the social background of foreigners in Germany. In particular, we look at the changing social provisions made for foreign workers in the light of their eventual change in status from temporary residents to de facto immigrants. A further factor in the changing social position of foreign workers has, of course, been the recent reunification of Germany; the repercussions of a unified Germany will also be a major topic of Chapter 2.

We turn to a consideration of the language of foreigners in Chapter 3. Here we undertake a detailed description of the structural and social characteristics of Foreign Worker German and investigate its status as a linguistic variety (or varieties), with reference to current work in pidgin and creole studies, language variation, and second-language-acquisition research. In our examination we consider data from my own observations, though primarily from the major German research projects, particularly the Heidelberger Forschungsprojekt Pidgindeutsch. We see that foreign workers also vary in the linguistic face they present. Variation can be detected across and within ethnic and linguistic groups, across time and generations, and, in fact, within individuals themselves. We see that, whereas there was originally profit to be gained from looking at universal characteristics of the language of foreign groups, it eventually emerged that the social interactional and personal communicative aspects of foreigner language are a far more fruitful, not to say socially responsible, focus of recent studies.

Variation across individuals, across groups, and across time is also a major theme of Chapter 4, which begins with an account of the development of foreigner literature. The main focus of this chapter is the way in which writers have used language to construct a series of different identities for themselves and the foreign community. We see that in the literature, as in the language, there has been a progression away from lumping all foreign writing together under a single heading *Gastarbeiterliteratur*. In fact, it emerges that foreign writers and a select few critics are now campaigning for foreign literature to be regarded not as exotic and foreign at all, but rather as a legitimate branch of German literature. This leads us to a consideration of the relationship between German insecurity about its own identity (since World War II and since reunification) and German attitudes toward foreigners and foreign literature. In so doing, we pay particular attention to the role of both the national and the minority intellectual elite in exploiting language as a symbol of group identity.

The general theoretical thrust of this book is a contemplation of the role of language in the negotiation and maintenance of individual and group identity. In particular, it examines the way in which language can be used as a tool to separate or unite people into different constellations, depending upon the social circumstances and the communicative task at hand. While all immigrant varieties of German can, at the will of the researcher, be lumped together as Foreign Worker German and while, indeed, a number of common characteristics can be isolated, there is in fact no such thing as a monolithic immigrant variety. Instead, immigrant German varies from speaker to speaker, from context to context, and from time to time.

Most importantly, however, as the ensuing chapters show, Foreign Worker German is being used to encode what Le Page and Tabouret-

Keller call "acts of identity"; that is to say, its use is frequently intended to express such social relations as Gastarbeiter vs. other foreigner, Gastarbeiter vs. German, Gastarbeiter vs. other worker, etc. In other words, Foreign Worker German is used to express power and solidarity relations, notions of ethnic identity, and other intangibles that are not usually the domain of a basic, instrumental pidgin used, for example, in trade and barter. Functionally, then, it is possible to argue that Foreign Worker German is expanding and that social conditions in Germany are ripe for this expansion, though, ultimately, definitions of pidgin and creole depend on a combination of social and linguistic factors:

> It has been proposed (Gilman 1979) that the significant difference between creoles and extended pidgins is not nativization, since the designation of what is a "first" as opposed to a "primary" language is arbitrary and irrelevant in many multilingual contexts, but rather whether the language is one of ethnic reference. However, this does not decide the issue of whether the differences between creoles and extended pidgins are entirely social rather than linguistic.
>
> (Holm 1988:7)

When one considers the *socio*linguistic dimensions of the issue, however, decisions are easier to make regarding the relationship between Foreign Worker German and other learner dialects. It is clear from the outset that Foreign Worker German does not operate in the same way as any other adult-learner dialect. Foreign Worker German takes on extremely important social functions, that is, it serves as a social semiotic (in the sense of M. A. K. Halliday), which leads us to a very different interpretation of its function. Foreign Worker German is used consciously and subconsciously in numerous specific and general social situations to mark ethnic and social identity, not just in terms of class, but in terms of perceived belonging and perceived difference. While one can hardly imagine, say, American relatives visiting Stuttgart, learning German in an informal setting, and defining themselves socially in terms of the learner language they speak, there is ample evidence to suggest that this is exactly what many foreign workers do with their version of German. Thus, regardless of the conclusion we reach on purely structural and strategic grounds, it all comes down to the same thing; it is essential to consider the social aspects of the definition of Foreign Worker German. It is exactly this highly visible social dimension that makes Foreign Worker German worthy of closer scrutiny.

Moreover, this sociofunctional as well as structural perception of Foreign Worker German helps one understand its status in Germany as a form of communication. It becomes not merely a symbol of incompetence in the use of Standard German, but also a signal of the other salient differences between foreign workers and mainstream Germans. One is reminded here of African American English: it displays a large number of linguistic features that are common to many other dialects, but the unique constellation of features, coupled with the social situations in which it is used, lead these same features to carry stigma when in the mouths of African Americans. By the same token, linguistic features approximating German that are considered positive or even endearing in the mouths, say, of British adults in a tourist setting are interpreted most negatively when incorporated in the utterances of foreign workers. In other words, we have here a classic illustration of a central sociolinguistic maxim, that value judgments about language are ultimately value judgments about the speakers themselves, not the language itself.

Just as we cannot lump their language forms together under one heading, so we cannot lump together the foreign workers themselves. Hinnenkamp (1990) has pointed out that a consequence of this lumping together of foreigners in Gastarbeiterlinguistik has been their inadvertent "ethnicization"—or, more precisely, "pan-ethnicization"—not on the basis of true ethnic characteristics, but rather according to shared social position and foreign experience. What is fascinating here is that it is exactly this kind of lumping together (*Vereinna(h)mung* "taking together/naming together") that causes shifts in group boundaries, compelling us to examine the consequences of ethnicization for Germans, foreign workers, and foreign writers.

The general direction of the book is informed by the theoretical themes of Pierre Bourdieu concerning language and power. Bourdieu argues that the ability to name and label people and things, a form of linguistic determinism, is a very powerful use of language, most clearly manifested in so-called "classification struggles." Bourdieu's treatment of symbolic struggles features the "strong social determinism of language use counterposed to a creativity of discourse at the group level, in struggles over definition and classification" (Collins 1993:124). There is never a perfect fit between the classification or label given and the social structure itself, and it is exactly this lag between the two that creates "room for negotiation" and allows for creative struggles over the classification itself. Moreover, struggles to change the representation, or the label, at these sites of conflict can also bring about actual change in the social structure, adjusting the amount of importance paid to particular traits, which are each invested with differing amounts of what Bourdieu has termed "capital" (to be understood as economic, cultural, social, or intellectual capital, as the context dictates). A classic recent example is the American struggle to define the "canon," which, giving the controversy a somewhat extreme interpretation, pits conservative, elitist representatives of a unifying culture against more practically oriented points of view that aim to train students to work in the real world. Perhaps, less extremely, we might interpret this debate as a site in which exclusionary practices are becoming more open to challenge.

Society is perpetually engaged in classification struggles, because the social structure is constantly changing and labeling cannot keep up with it. The outcome of these struggles has important consequences for group and, ultimately, for individual identity. As Bourdieu says with reference to conflict regarding job classifications:

> The fate of groups is bound up with the words that designate them. . . . the order of words never exactly reproduces the order of things. It is the relative independence of the structure of the system of classifying, classified words . . . in relation to the structure of the distribution of capital, and more precisely, it is the time-lag . . . between changes in jobs, linked to changes in the productive apparatus, and changes in titles, which creates the space for symbolic strategies aimed at exploiting the discrepancies between the nominal and the real.
>
> (1984:481)

Classification struggles are a central theme of each chapter of this book, though they manifest themselves rather differently in each field—the political, the linguistic, and the literary. What we see unfolding in the political history of immigration to Germany is a strategy of labeling by the German government that is intended to obscure the real social structure of immigrant labor in Germany. That is to say, by labeling all the foreign immigrants together as Gastarbeiter while at the same time insisting on the antilabel, that is, that Germany is not an immigration country, the government has sought more or less consciously to control the nature of its relationship to the workers it imports and (at least until recently) to ignore the needs of individuals. In other words, this labeling has always been a central strategy in Germany's political relationship toward foreign workers. By insisting on a label that conveys foreign workers' temporary status within the country ("*Gast*arbeiter") and by itself resisting the label "Einwanderungsland," the government has managed to deflect both its and society's attention away from the essential questions of integration and naturalization. We will see in Chapter 1 that this has been a deliberate strategy by the German government, even since the turn of the century.

Chapter 3 has as its central theme the classification by linguists of the language used by German foreign workers. Of course, the very nature of linguistic activity (the habitus of the linguist) is classificational: much linguistic work is expressly taxonomic. We see in the first part of this chapter that most of the early work on foreign-worker language was directed at finding a label for it as a whole: is it a pidgin, a creole, a learner dialect, or some other nameable variety? However, what indeed may have been carried out naively as a linguistic classificatory exercise has in fact had an inadvertent and largely negative social and political impact. As Hinnenkamp (1990) points out, by concentrating on the term "Gastarbeiterdeutsch" and by insisting on Gastarbeiterlinguistik as a subfield, linguists have caused (or at least have contributed to) the ethnicization of foreign workers as a group, once again drawing attention away from their individual differences and from the personal dimensions of their situation.

While this issue of "Vereinna(h)mung" concludes Chapter 3, it is taken up again expressly in Chapter 4, this time in the literary context. It is in the literary community that the classification struggle comes to a head and the strong links between the power of discourse and the distribution of capital become most evident. We see that, in the beginning, foreign writers accepted and exploited the labels "Gastarbeiter" and "Gastarbeiterliteratur" and addressed typical *Gastarbeiterthematik* ("guest worker themes") in their literary productions. A major reason for this was the need for solidarity, a sense of belonging, and a group identity, which itself tended to sacrifice actual group boundaries for the sake of stressing a shared experience, leading, for example, to the use of such slogans as *Jeder Gastarbeiter ist ein Türke* ("every Gastarbeiter is a Turk"). By accepting these labels imposed from elsewhere, foreign writers were able to accrue capital—cultural, intellectual, and, indeed, economic—and negotiate their identity as writers. However, as we shall demonstrate in Chapter 4, as time grew, just as Bourdieu predicts, the order of things changed in German society. Foreign workers became immigrants, and foreign writers needed to go beyond the typical themes of the Gastarbeiter experience and address other issues, widening their field of activity and, with this, their audience. It became increasingly clear that, without conforming to the Gastarbeiter label, there was no capital to be gained from literary activity: the presses would only publish works that dealt with Gastarbeiterthematik, which had proven itself a reliable seller with the customers. Hence, what developed was that lag between the label and the social structure, that essential space in which new labels are thrashed out and new identities forged. Echoing the "canon wars" of the United States, we are now witnessing the struggle by immigrant worker writers to slough off the title "Gastarbeiter," and to be accepted, not as foreigners *outside*, but as minority groups *within* the German mainstream. What is interesting is that, faced with this dilemma, immigrant writers have no place to go in their struggle for classification other than toward the mainstream. They have become so dissociated from their original identity (as Turkish Turk or Italian Italian) and so much a contributing part of German society (their whole habitus having changed) that they must negotiate for a German identity with a foreign substrate, rather than the other way around.

1. Guests and Immigrants: The Historical and Political Background

Introduction

Every society is a product of its history. In the case of Germany, a number of cataclysmic, as well as many less manifest, events of the last hundred years have defined attitudes toward foreign labor. Since linguists have often been criticized for ignoring the sociopolitical and economic background of their studies (Hinnenkamp 1990:283), we shall undertake to survey German social, economic, and political history here as it pertains to migrant labor in order to understand fully the effect of the past on the present linguistic and sociocultural situation of foreigners in Germany.

From the outset we note that foreign workers in Germany have always belonged to many different subgroups, so that it has always been very difficult to refer to them with one umbrella term. We also see that throughout the twentieth century Germany has refused to regard itself as an Einwanderungsland, in contrast to the United States, Australia, or Canada, and that the German government has always regarded the importation of labor as a temporary phenomenon. German policy toward foreigners has always been dictated by the market: more foreign labor in times of economic boom and less in times of bust. Hardly surprisingly, however, whenever there has been a large influx of foreigners to Germany, we detect a concomitant increase in tensions between them and the indigenous population.

The recent history of foreign labor in Germany can be defined as one long classification struggle of the type discussed by Bourdieu and described in the Introduction. The German government and its representatives constantly seek to impose a particular identity on the workers from abroad—as guests and not as immigrants—and to deny Germany's own identity as a country of immigration, thus effectively suppressing the right of the immigrants to negotiate their own identity and hampering the process of integration.

Foreign Labor from 1864 to the Present: A Historical Overview

Foreign Labor to 1945

The migration of labor to Germany is by no means a recent phenomenon: migrant labor has found employment in the German economy since the late 1800s. Once Polish peasants were freed in 1864, for example, large numbers of ethnic Polish[1] migrants and their families began to take seasonal employment regularly in the thriving German agriculture. They eventually settled in the industrial areas of central and western Germany and moved into piecework, which paid appreciably more than agricultural labor. This gradual westward migration produced a labor shortage in the east of the German empire, resulting in the importation of workers from Austrian Galicia. This importation was organized centrally for the first time in 1898 by the Ministry of Agriculture to help regulate recruitment and control the mistreatment of foreigners. Between 1900 and 1914 the number of migrant workers in Germany increased officially from 170,000 to 750,000, but in reality the increase was probably considerably higher on account of the simultaneous importation of illegal labor (*Rückblick* 1986:7–8). Castles and Kosack (1985:19) point out that in 1907 foreign workers constituted 4.1 percent of the total workforce in Germany. The number of foreign residents, including dependents, was listed in the 1910 census as 1,259,880.

Tensions between foreign workers and Germans led the German government in 1907 to introduce legislation to restrict the numbers of Poles in Germany. This included both a large-scale expulsion and the requirement that huge numbers of Poles leave Germany at Christmas every year so that they should not meet permanent residence requirements. Moreover, in 1908, linguistic legislation led to a ban on the public use of the Polish language. As a countermeasure, "dumb assemblies" were introduced by the Poles, in which leaflets printed in Polish were read together, but no one spoke a word (Castles and Kosack 1985: 20). Eventually, however, the Poles were assimilated into the local Ruhr population.

In the years before World War I a two-tiered agricultural and industrial economy developed in Germany. As is the case today, migrant workers carried out all of the harder and dirtier jobs that German workers were reluctant to do and that required little or no skill. By 1913, 164,100 out of a total of 409,900 Ruhr miners were thought to be ethnic Poles, though this figure included Poles with German citizenship (Castles and Kosack 1985:20). It was the sheer number of ethnic

Poles, it seems, that led to the tensions between them and the indigenous German workers. In particular, Castles and Kosack maintain that the Poles were feared and mistrusted by the Germans since they could be exploited because of their "ignorance of prevailing conditions" (that is, because they lived crowded together in substandard housing, which itself bred crime, disease, and social problems). Moreover, "[f]urther causes of conflict arose at the work-place itself. Foreigners had a high accident rate due to their frequent job changes, their inexperience in industry, and also because safety regulations in their own languages were usually lacking. They often worked harder and longer for less money than Germans, undermining improvements gained by the trade unions" (20).

With the outbreak of World War I the need for workers in the munitions and service industries increased significantly and migrant workers already working in Germany were barred from returning home. Predominantly Russo-Polish and Russian foreign workers took care of agriculture in the east of the country, while the Prusso-Polish workers from this area, who were officially regarded as *Reichsdeutsche* ("imperial Germans"), were requisitioned into the industrial areas in the west. From the very beginning, the presence of Polish migrant workers caused social problems in Germany; they were met with prejudice and resentment, in particular since a number of them failed to return to Poland, choosing instead to settle in the areas close to their work: the so-called *Ruhrpolen* (*Rückblick* 1986:9). The German Bureau of Industry also recruited workers from Belgium from the beginning of the war until the winter of 1917–18, but Belgian workers did not face the degree of resentment experienced by the Poles.

After World War I Germany shrank considerably in both physical area and industrial and economic capacity, and restrictions were consequently placed on migrant labor by the 1922 *Arbeitsnachweisgesetz* ("Employment Registration Law"), although a centralized, official recruitment organization was nevertheless maintained. Throughout the Weimar Republic migrant labor functioned only as a substitute and a buffer for the German economy, and the worldwide depression eventually brought an end to labor importation altogether.

The usual label for foreign workers in this period was *Fremdarbeiter* ("alien workers"), and in the 1930s the *Fremdarbeiterfrage* ("alien-workers question") took on a political and racist character. As the economy came under Nazi totalitarian control, the number of foreign workers gradually decreased. By the beginning of World War II there were approximately 300,000 foreign workers in Germany, though this number does not include naturalized Polish immigrants.

During World War II only a small proportion of foreign labor in Germany was voluntary, these workers coming mainly from Austria and Italy. Forced labor was generally carried out by men and women from the occupied areas (*Rückblick* 1986:10–11). Castles and Kosack point out that during the war 11 million German men were removed from the workforce and that, by September 1944, 7.5 million foreign laborers were working in the Reich (1985:23). While it would be inappropriate here to go into detail about the extremes of Nazi behavior toward foreigners during World War II, Castles and Kosack bring out a number of the basic principles of Nazi treatment of foreign workers that have found an echo in the conduct of the postwar government. They cite Sauckel, the plenipotentiary for labor in Nazi Germany, who demanded of foreign laborers that "[a]ll the men must be fed, sheltered and treated in such a way as to exploit them to the highest possible extent at the lowest conceivable expenditure." And they make particular reference to Nazi treatment of East Europeans:

> ... Nazi ideology prescribed specially bad treatment for the Poles and Russians. Like the Jews they were compelled to wear badges showing their origin. Their housing was very poor and their food rations were so low that many died of starvation. While civilian workers from the west had the same wages and conditions as Germans (at least in theory), a special tax was levied on "Ostarbeiter" (Russians) and Poles to make clear the social difference between them and the Germans, as well as to keep down the living standards in the occupied area. After deductions for board and lodging, Poles and Russians received virtually no payment for their forced labor.
>
> (24)

Hence we see that the official German concept of immigrant labor since the turn of the century has been as a temporary phenomenon, as a commodity to be exploited in times of economic expansion and returned in times of hardship. Up until World War II, Germany recruited a variety of workers from different countries, who were united only by their shared experiences in Germany. No provisions were made to integrate these foreign workers into German society, and, instead, they were considered a disposable commodity and often regarded as a threat by the indigenous population. These same policies and tensions are echoed in more recent history.

Post–World War II Foreign Labor

Castles and Kosack have pointed out the major "pull" factors that have attracted migrant workers to certain Western European countries since the end of World War II and the "push" factors that have led to their leaving their home countries. The "pull" factors include economic growth linked with a shortage of labor caused by the high death rate in the war, the general aging of the population, improvements in education, and promotion within the labor force. The "push" factors include unemployment, poverty, and underdevelopment (1985:26–27). While these factors apply equally well to foreign labor in any of the other Western European countries, it has been suggested that what primarily differentiates migration to Germany is "its late beginning, its extremely rapid growth, and its character as highly organized labor migration" (39).

In a recent article on foreign workers and German policy toward foreigners, Karl-Heinz Meier-Braun (1995:16–19) divides foreign-worker history into four phases. The phase from 1955 to 1973 he calls the *Anwerbephase* ("recruitment phase"). From 1973 to 1979 is the *Konsolidierung der Ausländerbeschäftigung* ("consolidation of foreign labor"). The phase spanning the years from 1981 to 1990 is characterized by a change in immigration policy and the struggle for a new immigration law. The most recent phase, from 1990 to 1995 is characterized by Bade (1994: 66) as putting asylum policy in the foreground and largely forgetting foreign workers. In what follows, we will broadly sketch each of these four phases of German foreign-worker policy.

The Recruitment Phase

In 1946 industrial production was reduced to 30 percent of its 1938 capacity and agricultural production was reduced to 72 percent (Bade 1983:59), but Germany was able to cover its immediate workforce needs by incorporating into the economy about 7.8 million expellees (*Vertriebene*) from areas in the east that had previously been German territories (for example, the Sudetenland) but were annexed by Poland or the Soviet Union after 1945. Once production began to recover from World War II, however, the number of foreign workers grew dramatically, owing to a general dearth of Germans in the 12–35 year old age group, a 40 percent decrease in the birthrate, and an increase in the number of Germans of pensionable age. The native population decreased, leading to a skewed age distribution, with a large elderly population and few children.

The surge of economic prosperity in 1948, referred to as the *Wirt-*

schaftswunder (the "economic miracle"), led to an increasing number of job vacancies, owing to burgeoning wealth and the concurrent decrease in the number of women in the workforce. Until the erection of the Berlin Wall, another 3 million people immigrated into West Germany from East Germany (Lichtenberger 1984:72). After 1961, the influx of workers from East Germany stopped, however, leaving an even bigger gap in the labor force. According to Jones, the working population of West Germany declined by 800,000 between 1960 and 1970 as a consequence of normal aging, while the upward mobility of the better educated indigenous population also caused a further labor shortage in the more menial occupations (1983:72). The general improvement in working conditions across the economy also made Germans reluctant to take low-end jobs in heavy industry (such as coal mining) and in the service industries (such as cleaning and catering). Furthermore, a general reduction in the length of the working day also caused an increased demand for workers (*Rückblick* 1986:12–13).

The rapid improvement in the German economy proved very attractive to foreigners, who were now migrating from south to north instead of from east to west. By 1955 there were approximately 80,000 foreign workers in Germany, of which Italians represented the majority with 7,500 workers. In the years that followed, and in consultation with German trade unions, West Germany drew up foreign-worker recruitment contracts with less-developed countries as follows: Italy (1955), Spain (1960), Greece (1960), Turkey (1961 and 1964), Portugal (1964), Tunisia (1965), and Yugoslavia (1968) (Bundesministerium 1989a 1:9).

It has been suggested by sociologists, social economists, and social geographers that the German government regarded the recruitment of foreign workers as an easy way to deal with the inequities of a labor market in which unemployment levels were as low as 2.2 percent in Baden-Württemberg and 2.9 percent in North Rhine-Westphalia in 1955 (average unemployment rate, 5.1 percent), but as unnervingly high as 11.2 percent in Schleswig-Holstein. While the second world war had seen the destruction of only 6 percent of industrial machinery and as little as 17 percent of a total industrial capacity that had expanded dramatically during the war years, its most significant outcome was damage to approximately 80 percent of domestic dwellings. The priority after the war was clearly economic reconstruction to the detriment of social policies. As a consequence it was deemed more expedient to import foreign labor on a short-term basis and house foreign workers in inferior housing, especially in old barracks, rather than to have to build new housing to facilitate the relocation of unemployed, indigenous German workers (Herbert 1990:202). Moreover, it appears that the importation of foreign labor permitted a curb to be placed on wage demands from local workers, particularly in agriculture, since the gross shortage of workers had driven up wage levels and threatened to increase them still further (205).

It would, however, be simplistic to argue that economic and housing issues alone motivated the importation of foreign labor. Undoubtedly, a positive spin can be put on the argument for the importation of labor; indeed, it was originally believed that the system would be of direct benefit both to the foreign workers themselves and to their home countries. They would enjoy paid employment when none was available at home, and they would receive technical training, which they could use on their return from Germany, thus increasing the expertise available in their home countries. Moreover, they would earn West German currency that they could send home to improve general conditions and to establish places of employment for themselves on their return, while at the same time increasing their immediate standard of living.

Implicit in all of these beliefs was the idea that foreign workers would not be a permanent feature of the German labor market. Throughout this period it was stressed time and again that Germany was not an immigration country ("Deutschland ist kein Einwanderungsland") and that foreign labor would only be profitable if it were a short-term proposition. Consequently, the foreign worker was denied the right to stay for longer than two or three years in Germany. This principle is reflected in the term used for the workers themselves, that is, *guest*, not *immigrant*, workers. They were considered *Gäste auf Abruf* ("guests on call")[2] and were treated accordingly. Since they were only in Germany to work and earn money before returning home again, no provision was made for the workers to bring their families with them or to learn German in a formal setting. They had not come to settle and socialize or to be integrated into West German society. Indeed, as we shall see below, this principle of rotation has lasted far beyond even the recruitment ban of 1973 and persists today, allowing German industry to import labor for specific, short periods of time and guaranteeing that workers will return home at the end of the original term of their visa (Meier-Braun 1995:18–19).

It was not only the German government and the government of the recruitment countries that favored a time limit on foreign labor in Germany. Foreign workers themselves intended to earn as much money as possible in a short space of time and then immediately return home. However, as the German government gradually extended the duration of their stay, and as their own aspirations remained unfulfilled, foreign workers eventually, though often reluctantly, came around to the idea that they would need to stay in Germany for a greater length of time. The result was a dramatic increase in the number of foreign workers in Germany. In 1960 there had been approximately 280,000 foreign workers in Germany (50 percent of whom were Italians, as well as 13,000 Greeks, 9,400 Spaniards, 8,800 Yugoslavs, and 2,500 Turks). As the economy grew it became increasingly difficult to fill the labor gap; as a consequence the number of foreign workers solicited by organized recruitment expanded dramatically. Thus, the number of foreign workers reached 1.2 million by 1965 and 2.6 million by 1973, and, when one includes the families that were eventually allowed to join the workers, the total number of foreigners in the Federal Republic in the 1970s eventually surpassed 4 million (*Rückblick* 1986:16).

From 1960 onward the Federal Labor Institute maintained recruitment centers in the most important source countries to prescreen applicants, the majority of whom came from agricultural areas and were consequently eligible only for unskilled or semiskilled positions. In 1973 foreign workers made up about 12 percent of the total West German workforce, though in certain occupations they were more strongly represented: 21.9 percent in the building industry; 20 percent in rubber, plastics, and asbestos processing; 20.5 percent in the hotel trade; and 17 percent in other service industries. In contrast to conditions in the first decades of the twentieth century, however, only 1 percent of foreigners were employed in agriculture (*Rückblick* 1986:17). Throughout the 1980s and into the 1990s, up to 80 percent of foreigners have continued to be employed in positions that Germans are reluctant to fill. In mining, for example, the first group of foreign workers were Italians. However, once Italian workers were able to progress into other, more desirable industrial and service positions, these mining positions were filled first by Spanish, then by Dutch, Belgian, and French workers. By the 1960s, since almost no other group remained that was willing to work in the moribund mining industry, Turks alone for the most part were recruited to do this work (*Rückblick* 1986:17).

The advantage to German business of importing foreign labor into the German economy has been primarily economic. By importing labor, the postwar labor shortage, which was causing wages to skyrocket and was thus especially hurting middle-ranking concerns, could be brought under control. Moreover, foreign labor was seen as a way to cover the less challenging and more physically strenuous positions, which were becoming increasingly difficult to fill with indigenous labor. The foreign-worker solution also lessened the burden on industry and commerce to provide better working conditions, child-care facilities, part-time employment, job-sharing programs, etc., which would attract mothers and other members of the population who might otherwise not be able or willing to join the workforce (*Rückblick* 1986:18).

Anyone reading Wallraff's *Industriereportagen* very quickly gets a clear picture—exaggerated or not—of the negative social impact of importing foreign labor. This development is not atypical of the rest of Europe and has led more than one commentator to suggest that the major role of foreign workers, not just in Germany, but in all of developed Western Europe, is to form a new *Lumpenproletariat* (Skutnabb-Kangas 1984) or a special "underclass" (Skutnabb-Kangas 1981b; Kolodny 1977:218) as a buffer for indigenous workers, who would use them as a springboard to improved employment opportunities and conditions on the one hand, and blame them for any adverse conditions on the other. In this way, the onus is taken off government and industry and the home population itself, both economically and financially, while at the same time the home government can boast of its social conscience and general altruism, since it is offering employment to the disadvantaged citizens of less prosperous and developing countries.

There are social economists and geographers who argue explicitly that the social structure of Germany underwent this kind of *Unterschichtung*—the development of a subproletariat—in the 1950s and 1960s (for example, Herbert 1990). This new underclass allowed the local population to be rationalized away from undesirable positions. Such jobs, which require and provide little or no training and little or no opportunity for promotion or general improvement in pay and conditions, certainly lay the groundwork for a cycle of poverty in the foreign-worker population.

In the 1950s and 1960s, then, a two-tier labor economy developed, reminiscent of that in the World War I years, but industrial rather than agricultural in nature. In those areas employing a high proportion of foreign workers, chances of promotion and general improvement were slim, in contrast to other sectors of the labor market. Moreover, traditional foreign-worker positions were easy prey to the exigencies of a fluctuating market. For this reason also foreign employment could be said to fulfill a substitute and buffer function, *Ersatz- und Pufferfunktion* (*Rückblick* 1986:18–19). The *Ausländergesetz* ("foreigners law") of 28 April 1965 stipulated that everyone wishing to work in the Federal Republic was required to have both a residency permit and a work permit. This led to a Catch-22 situation for foreigners: without a work permit they could not get a job, and without a job they could not get a work permit. This is a very simple system of control that has been used effectively by a number of governments to regulate the influx of foreign labor. Moreover, when EEC member countries introduced greater freedom and protection for their citizens between the years 1961 and 1970, this merely resulted in Germans opting to employ more Yugoslavs and Turks, who did not come under the protection of the law (Hamm 1988:26).

Even on economic grounds the importation of foreign labor was not without its critics. With the recession in 1966-67, it was suggested that foreign labor was holding back industrial mechanization by keeping jobs open that could be carried out more efficiently by machines. Furthermore, foreign workers were beginning to demand better housing and other improvements in their living standards, which cost money and therefore rendered foreign labor less profitable. On the whole, however, the use of foreign workers was defended by government officials (for example, by Economics Minister Schiller) and others as being of real benefit to the economy, particularly since it gave German employers the flexibility to hire more foreign workers in times of economic boom and fewer in times of bust.

It must also be noted that from the seventies onward it became more common for large companies to export their capital out of Europe, rather than invest in foreign labor within European countries. Since foreign workers were now demanding better conditions, it was more profitable to export capital to countries with "masses of willing, cheap, unorganized labor and advantageous tax laws," such as Portugal and Latin America, than to import labor to Western industrialized countries (Skutnabb-Kangas 1986:168-69).

Until the 1970s the federal government was careful to cover the labor shortage with foreign workers according to the demands of employers, often to the detriment of social programs meant for these same foreign workers, although poor worker conditions were gradually becoming a political issue in Germany. In 1971 the German government attempted to place an initial check on the importation of foreign labor by introducing a dated-entry system (*Einreisesichtvermerk*) for the first time. This was in response to a call for a limitation on immigration in light of the internal educational, social, and cultural problems it was now seen to be creating.

The Consolidation Phase

The number of nonworking foreigners increased sharply from 137,200 in 1961 to 1.37 million in 1973, strongly indicating the trend for foreign nationals to settle in Germany on a long-term or permanent basis. In particular, some Germans found it disturbing that families were joining the foreign workers in Germany, thus increasing the tendency for them to stay on. This led to a number of stringent governmental measures to curb immigration and to reduce the "economic burden" of the foreign residents. New immigration and labor laws were adopted in an attempt to curb the trend, eventually culminating, on 23 November 1973, in a complete ban on recruitment, the so-called *Anwerbestopp*. While this measure was not introduced as a direct result of the oil crisis, the worldwide recession certainly gave it greater impetus. West Germany's reaction to the recession was similar to that of other European countries at the time: reduced quotas, restrictions on the number of foreign workers allowed in and on their length of stay, and a ban on recruitment (Lichtenberger 1984:77).

Hitherto it had been possible for foreign workers to return home and, after a time, seek renewed employment in Germany. Ironically, however, once it was forbidden to enter Germany in order to take up employment, those foreign workers already in Germany tended to stay for longer periods of time, most often ten years or more. Coupled with measures introduced to guarantee human rights, encourage stability, and promote the unification of families (*Familiennachzug*) (Jones 1983: 77), the new labor laws allowed more and more family members to join their working relatives in Germany, causing an overall increase in the foreign population despite the ban on new recruitment. Foreign women in particular joined the German workforce in large numbers at this time, particularly in the "typically female" personal services, such as the hospitality trade and cleaning (Lichtenberger 1984:79). Given these developments, it is not surprising that almost 70 percent of the children of foreign workers in Germany were born there (*Rückblick* 1986:20). Speaking of the years of consolidation, Castles and Kosack talk in terms of the end of the "guest worker system" and a complete restructuring of the foreign population: "[t]he shift from a temporary migrant labor force to a permanent ethnic minority is a complex process that relies upon the character of the original recruitment. In Germany it is clearly the case that the unplanned, provisional and make-do nature of the original immigration is now taking its toll on the minorities who have made Germany their permanent home" (1985:489).

Changes in Immigration Policy

At the end of the consolidation phase, in 1979, Heinz Kuhn, the first *Ausländerbeauftragter* ("commissioner for foreigners") of the Federal Republic, criticized government policy toward foreigners and demanded the recognition of the *faktische Einwanderung* ("de facto immigration") of the foreign workers in the form of communal voting rights. The federal government ignored this suggestion and did nothing about another issue Kuhn had stressed, that of facilitating citizenship claims for young foreigners (Meier-Braun 1995:17). Instead, it was deemed that the main problem was that the number of foreigners living in Germany was still too high, which ultimately ushered in a long phase of foreigner policy, from 1981 to 1991, during which limiting the number of foreigners was the top priority.

After much political wrangling, in particular about the upper age for admitting children of foreign workers, the *Gesetz zur Förderung der Rückkehrbereitschaft von Ausländern* (literally, "law to promote foreigners' willingness to return") was passed on 10 October 1983. To claimants who were unemployed after 20 October 1983 or who had been working part-time during the previous six months and who were willing to return home with their whole family, this law provided the sum of 10,500 DM per adult and 1,500 DM per child, payable in the home country. A time limit (30 June 1984), was placed on these claims, but by February 1984 more than 150,000 claims had been lodged, the majority of them by Turkish workers (Lichtenberger 1984:81).

During this period, which included, crucially, a change in government from the SPD-FDP coalition to the conservative CDU-CSU-FDP coalition in the middle of 1983, it is clear that there was a tendency to politicize the whole foreigner issue. Despite the fact that much political capital was made out of the issue, no plan for changes in the foreigners law was given really serious consideration until the spring of 1988, when the Bundesinnenministerium, the Federal Office of the Interior or Home Office, circulated a widely criticized draft proposing further restrictions on immigration. It came as a surprise to the government that the proposed new restrictions were met by a unified front of resistance by churches and charities, the commissioner for foreigners, the workers' and employers' unions, interest groups, the media, and the parliamentary opposition, as well as the liberal FDP faction and even the left wing of the CDU. This outcry was partially responsible for a cabinet reshuffle.

The surge of antiforeigner activity and the success of the right-wing radical parties in Berlin and the communal elections had acted as a loud wake-up call to many Germans. In September 1989, Liselotte Funcke, then Ausländerbeauftragte, warned of the dangers of extremist activities in the absence of a new foreigner policy. That same month, Wolfgang Schäuble, the recently appointed *Bundesinnenminister* ("federal minister of the interior"), finally proposed a new immigration law, which reached the Bundesrat by 11 May 1990 and came into effect on 1 January 1991.

The new law, which made a number of relatively small changes, was not generally considered to be a vast improvement on the old law. While it did make the ban on recruitment official, Paragraph 10 nevertheless actually allows for new recruitment under the rotation principle for a limited time. That is to say, it allows for the temporary recruitment of labor to fill in gaps in the workforce. A further major objection to this new law persists, especially within the FDP, that it still does not regulate residency issues clearly, particularly with reference to young foreigners and since it lacks provisions for guaranteed residency for the spouse of a foreign worker. A final important weakness is that the new law to this day fails to provide administrative guidelines; it has been described as *Verschärfungen durch die Hintertür* ("tightening up via the back door")(Meier-Braun 1995:18-19).

Asylum Seekers, Refugees, and Foreign Workers

The question of residency and citizenship rights remains a matter of highly controversial debate in Germany today. Its importance to long-term foreign workers and their children is so great that we will subsequently discuss this question in greater depth. To understand the full extent of the residency/citizenship debate in the Federal Republic, however, we first need to examine how the waters of foreign-worker policy have been muddied considerably in recent years by the asylum question in Germany, as indeed in the rest of Europe.

Partly in reaction to the horrors perpetrated against foreigners under Hitler, Article 16 of the *Grundgesetz* of 1949 guaranteed asylum to the politically persecuted without qualification—*Politisch Verfolgte genießen Asylrecht* ("the politically persecuted have the right to asylum"). Coupled with Germany's geographical position in the center of Europe and the economic leadership it would soon enjoy, it was all but guaranteed that Germany would become a primary destination for people seeking political asylum.

In particular, this very liberal policy has encouraged great numbers of asylum seekers and refugees to enter the Federal Republic in the past decade, and the problem has become much more acute since reunification.

In the last five years much attention has been paid to the refugees and asylum seekers in the international media. There are now close to 2 million refugees in the Federal Republic, almost 400,000 of whom arrived

Table 1. Country of Origin of Refugees, 1989–1992

Poland	16.0%
Yugoslavia	14.8%
Turkey	13.6%
Romania	9.3%
Lebanon	6.3%
Iran	4.9%
Sri Lanka	4.0%
Afghanistan	2.5%
Vietnam	2.5%

Source: Grosch 1992:143

in Germany in the period from 1989 to 1992. About 75 percent of the refugees originated from nine specific countries, as shown in Table 1.

Since *perestroika* and the breakup of the Soviet Union, fewer refugees have been accepted from former Eastern Bloc countries. Instead, people from Third World countries have come to constitute a significant group of refugees, escaping not just political, but also religious persecution, as well as civil war, terror, poverty, and famine. While only 10 percent of applicants were and are ultimately accepted in Germany as bona fide political refugees, the original Article 16 of the constitution stated that even those who are not eligible for *political* refugee status cannot be returned home "because Germany is bound by national and international laws and principles to grant them help and protection for humanitarian reasons." As a consequence, about 60 percent of all refugees were classified as "de facto refugees," though they are often regarded by the general public as "economic refugees" or even as "cheats" just looking for a better life (Grosch 1992:144).

In late 1991 the German asylum issue reached international attention when the first wave of violence against asylum seekers occurred. The tide soon turned against foreign workers as well, as will be discussed in Chapter 2. Once again, it appears that the sheer numbers of refugees involved triggered political and popular reaction. In 1991 an astronomical 256,112 refugees arrived in the Federal Republic, provoking a wave of hysteria among German politicians and antiforeigner campaigns in a number of places. Two polls at the end of 1991 indicated a general change in the attitudes of Germans toward asylum seekers. According to an Allensbach survey, 69 percent of West Germans and 64 percent of East Germans wanted a constitutional amendment regarding refugees; a Politbarometer poll showed that 71 percent of West Germans —

though only 16 percent of East Germans—regarded the asylum issue as Germany's most pressing problem (Grosch 1992:147–48). Grosch considers three factors as causing the acuteness of the refugee issue:

> The collapse of communism and particularly the aftermath of unification have created an atmosphere of such uncertainty that decision-making seems to have been paralysed. This has led to a general erosion of confidence in established politicians and parties.
>
> The current tense social and economic situation in eastern Germany, added to the traditionally provincial attitudes on the part of many Germans . . . , have led to increased antagonism towards foreigners now that money is tight and a lot more foreigners are asking for help (which many see as a costly handout).
>
> Germany is reputed to be a nation low on self-confidence. Certainly the present approach to foreigners and the refugee problem would indicate that there is some truth to this. Even before the country has had time to redefine its post-unification national identity, politicians are pushing hard for political union on a European level, requiring yet another identity redefinition. Insecurity is rampant.
>
> (148)

The situation was exacerbated by the record influx of 438,191 refugees to Germany in 1992 alone, many of whom entered from the former Yugoslavia (Bade 1994:98).

Chancellor Kohl's first interparty meeting on the issue did not lead to a constitutional amendment, but rather to an agreement to speed up the processing of refugee petitions, to an average processing time of six weeks. In the March 1992 state elections in Baden-Württemberg and Schleswig-Holstein the asylum problem was a major campaign issue, and it led to right-wing fringe parties gaining ground on the basis of a "Germany for the Germans" policy (*Deutschland den Deutschen*). There were repeated calls by politicians to amend Article 16, often on the grounds that Germany simply could not cope with the influx. For example, Glos, the chairman of the CSU regional party insisted that Germany is "kein Einwanderungsland. . . . Die Aufnahmekapazität unseres Landes und unsere[r] Bevölkerung darf nicht überfordert werden. Wer dies tut, fördert Fremdenfeindlichkeit"[3] (*Frankfurter Allgemeine Zeitung*, 27 May 1993).

The law on asylum was finally changed on 26 May 1993 and a new Article 16a added, which permitted border officials to turn back asylum seekers from countries where it was deemed that there was no political persecution and to return refugees attempting entry from bordering countries (Poland, Czechoslovakia, Austria, and Switzerland) and "safe third countries" (*sichere Drittländer*) such as those in Scandinavia, where human rights and basic freedoms are guaranteed. In addition, the German government intends to return refugees from the former Yugoslavia once the conflict is over (*Frankfurter Allgemeine Zeitung*, 27 May 1993; Bade 1994:124). Thus we see that this phase of policy is dominated by efforts to restrict the numbers; concomitantly, emphasis has clearly shifted from measures to integrate those foreigners already in Germany to preventing any more from coming in.

Foreigners in the German Democratic Republic

While the asylum issue is of grave concern to the whole of the industrialized world, the added problems of reunification are, of course, unique to Germany. In this section, we focus on two major issues emerging from the unification of West and East Germany. First, there is the question of what types of foreigners were in the German Democratic Republic and what its relationship to them was before unification. Second, we need to discuss how unification has had an impact on the relationship between ex-citizens of the German Democratic Republic and foreigners throughout the united Federal Republic, occasionally placing these groups in direct competition with each other.

While the former German Democratic Republic did not witness immigration to the same extent that West Germany did, there were nevertheless immigrants who chose to live there for personal or political reasons. Most of them were foreigners *auf Zeit* ("short term"), who had been delegated by their home countries, which were allied with the GDR, to go there for a specific reason, though an officially unspecified number did choose to make the GDR their "second home" or "home of choice" (Hexelschneider 1989:350–51). In 1989, 166,419 foreign citizens over the age of eighteen and from a total of 129 different countries lived in the GDR. Of these, 33,789 had permanent residence, more than 85,000 were workers, and more than 12,600 were students.

Foreigners thus were divided roughly into two groups: students and workers, who were living in the GDR for a longer or shorter period in order to obtain further qualifications. Students and workers both were more likely to have gone to East Germany as a result of a reciprocal agreement between the GDR and their home country. According to Bade (1994:178), in 1989 the majority of foreigners in the GDR were employed in factories, including 59,000 Vietnamese and 15,000 Mozambicans. Bade points out that the official government policy was to segregate these workers from the rest of East German society, so that there were fewer problems of integration than might be expected largely because integration was officially out of the question. The plight of the large numbers of stranded Vietnamese workers since reunification has recently been the subject of newspaper reports both in Germany and throughout the rest of the world. The majority of foreign students in the GDR came from socialist countries, most commonly from Vietnam, Cuba, Algeria, Hungary, Poland, other parts of Africa, and South-East Asia (Hexelschneider 1989:351).

In contrast to the situation in the Federal Republic, every employee resident in the GDR on the basis of an international agreement was required to take an intensive course in German. Accordingly, in 1962 the Zentrale Schule für ausländische Bürger zur sprachlichen Vorbereitung auf die produktionstechnische Ausbildung ("Central School of Linguistic Preparation for Training in Production Techniques for Foreign Citizens") was established in Dresden-Radebeul, becoming part of the Herder Institute in 1968. Courses were also available for students who had not learned sufficient German for their studies in their home countries, and the central organization for this was the Institut für Ausländerstudium der Karl-Marx-Universität Leipzig ("Institute for Foreign Students of the Karl Marx University in Leipzig"), founded in 1956, which also became part of the Herder Institute, in 1961. There was also a four-semester-long companion course in German for Foreigners during the regular academic course, which concentrated on technical German and came under the auspices of the Institut für Deutsche Fachsprache ("Institute for Technical German") at the Technical University of Dresden (Hexelschneider 1989:351).

Apart from language studies, foreign students in the GDR could maintain their national culture while learning about German culture and politics through a number of organizations and initiatives organized at the official level, and there were a number of clubs and organizations run by the foreign nationals themselves, as well as international student committees. A network of official work brigades at the various factories also organized the foreign workers, many of whom were youths (Hexelschneider 1989:354).

Finally, on 6 March 1989, a law was passed which gave voting rights in municipal elections to all foreign citizens over the age of eighteen who had an official work and permanent-residency permit and had been in the GDR for longer than six months (Hexelschneider 1989:354). While these measures most certainly did not eradicate discrimination and xenophobia, they certainly went a long way toward containing the problem of foreign residents until unification.

As we will see in Chapter 2 in greater detail, shortly after unification acts of aggression against foreigners became very common in the states of the former GDR. Indeed, the first wave began with the attack on a home for asylum seekers in Hoyerswerda in August 1991, followed shortly by the attacks in Rostock-Lichtenhagen. While it was soon clear that violence against foreigners is not exclusive to the former GDR states, there is no question that this part of Germany witnesses an astonishing amount of it.

A number of reasons for this xenophobia have been suggested. First, there have always been many fewer foreigners in eastern than in western Germany, and these numbers have even dropped dramatically since unification. Second, under the old SED regime foreigners lived for the most part isolated from the rest of the population. Moreover, it has been suggested that peaceful coexistence with foreigners had been legislated in the old GDR and that, once unification occurred, this approach was rejected along with many other socialist features. Instead of this legislative coexistence, a "gloomy nationalism" developed to compensate for East Germans' lost political identity, and this developed into dislike and even hatred of foreigners. However, a worse factor even than this is the general uncertainty that has gripped the former GDR since unification, as it has undergone sweeping changes in policy, economy, and social structure. The high unemployment rate in the former socialist states is particularly significant here, since it gives East Germans (especially less educated youth) the impression that they are vying directly with foreigners for jobs and social benefits, even when they are not. On top of this, it has been suggested that the former well-organized (if compulsory) way of life of East German youth has now given way to a complete lack of community and social organization. "Dangerous boredom" has led to some of the xenophobic activity (Aktion Gemeinsinn 1993).

Aussiedler

The so-called *Aussiedler* (a term that is very hard to translate; it means approximately "returning settlers") constitute a group of new residents in Germany who were not born there, but have received German citizenship on the grounds that they are related by blood to "Germans" who left the German-speaking area to settle in a number of colonies in the eighteenth and nineteenth centuries.[4] Since, technically, they receive German passports on entry and are not classified by the Germans as foreigners, I have not included them in the category of foreign workers in this study. However, it is becoming increasingly clear that they are also experiencing severe hostility from their distant German "cousins." Indeed, recently on a brief trip to Germany, I was told at least three times that the Aussiedler were *the* most vexing group of foreigners in Germany today. Malchow, Tayebi, and Brand (1990) and Bade (1994) provide very good discussions of their history and current status.

Suffice it to say here that, politically, the Aussiedler are an important group. The fact that they fulfill (albeit remotely) the *ius sanguinis* ("law of the blood") criterion has been enough to secure them official status as Germans from the point of view of the government, even if it has not been sufficient to gain them acceptance in the eyes of mainstream Germans. Thus, their current and future position is a complicating factor in the cultural debate about what it means to be German. Linguistically this group is also very interesting, since many Aussiedler claim to speak German; this ability, in fact, is one important criterion for their official acceptance into Germany. However, it is generally clear that Aussiedler German is wholly inadequate to meet its speakers' everyday needs and that, in fact, it often amounts to no more than the knowledge of a few sayings and other linguistic formulae, along with a song or a poem or two. While research on this group is in its earliest stages, the Aussiedler need to be observed closely, since they will have an important impact on the language and identity issues that are central in this work.

Citizenship/Dual Citizenship for Resident Foreigners

Since the unification of Germany, it has been notoriously difficult for the German Federal Bureau of Statistics to provide reliable demographic information. Bearing in mind, then, that the situation in the Federal Republic is more fluid now than ever owing to the relaxed restrictions on immigration to Germany from a large number of other countries (mostly East European), we can get an idea from the latest available statistics, displayed in Figure 1, of the predominant nationalities of immigrants in Germany. It should also be borne in mind that a large group of immigrants, the *Volksdeutsche* from Kazakhstan, Russia, Poland, and other former Eastern Bloc states, all receive German citizenship upon arrival and therefore do not appear in statistics about foreigners.

According to Bade (1994:57) the current phase of German foreigner policy, beginning in 1990, has been obscured by considerable overlap between the debate on long-term resident foreign workers and the asylum seeker/refugee issue. Meier-Braun suggests that, while the protagonists may have changed, little has been learned from the past, and the story is still the same: "Die politische Auseinandersetzung und die Schlagzeilen in den Medien sind beinahe austauschbar: Man

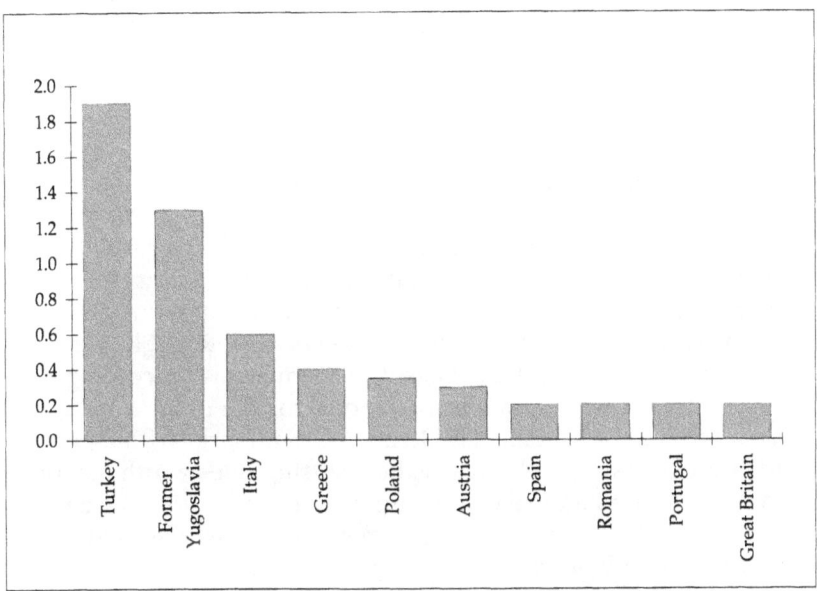

Figure 1. Foreigners Living in Germany, by Nationality (in millions, end of 1994)

braucht nur 'Türken' durch 'Asylbewerber' zu ersetzen. In beiden Fällen drohte das 'volle Boot Bundesrepublik Deutschland' durch die angeblich zu hohen Zahlen der—damals Türken bzw.—heute—Flüchtlinge und Asylsuchenden zu kippen"[5] (1995:19). Meier-Braun is quite cynical about the "new" debate on foreigners that has followed the 1993 amendment of Article 16 of the Basic Law:

> Die Parallele zwischen den Türken damals und den Asylsuchenden heute macht auch deutlich, wie wenig aus der ausländerpolitischen Debatte gelernt wurde. Zu Beginn der achtziger Jahre lebte etwa eine Million Türken in Deutschland, deren Zahl angeblich zu verringern galt. Heute sind es fast doppelt so viele, was nun offenbar keine Rolle mehr spielt. Kaum jemand erinnert sich noch an diesen Zusammenhang oder an Zitate von verantwortlichen Politikern wie "Es kommt, solange ich in Hessen was zu sagen habe, kein Türke mehr ins Land." Das gilt auch für den Satz eines anderen Politikers, der sagte: "Mein Ziel ist die Lösung eines Ausländerproblems, das im wesentlichen türkische Familien betrifft."[6]

(19)

However, as Grosch (1992:144) has pointed out, foreign workers who were called to Germany to work, together with their families, make up the majority of the over six and a half million foreigners in the country today. Now that it is clear they are not going home, the German government is faced with finding ways to acculturate them and to establish ways in which native and nonnative Germans can live together without fear of a repetition of antiforeigner incidents such as those in Hoyerswerda, Mölln, and Solingen. Crucial here are the related questions of foreign-born workers acquiring German citizenship and of their children receiving dual citizenship; at the time of writing, both of these subjects remain hotly disputed in the Federal Republic. Citizenship for the long-term foreign residents in Germany is proceeding very haltingly, despite proclamations of support for the process by politicians. In 1993, for example, only Berlin and Hamburg (with 2 percent and 1 percent, respectively) reached citizenship rates worth mentioning, while Bavaria had the lowest naturalization rates with 0.4 percent (Thränhardt 1995:3). As we have seen, many foreign workers have lived in Germany for a long time: the average residency in 1995 was twenty years; many of these individuals belong to the second or third generation of resident workers and were, perhaps, also born in Germany.

Citizenship continues to be extremely difficult to obtain in the Federal Republic. Recent law permitted foreign workers to apply for citizenship only after fifteen years of permanent residence, and applications had to be made by 1995. Citizenship is then only granted "if it is not against the interests of the Federal Republic" (Grosch 1992:139). Furthermore, there are numerous citizenship constraints on the children of foreigners since federal citizenship laws operate on the basis of *ius sanguinis*, as opposed to *ius solis* ("law of the soil"). Again, according to the new foreigners law, children between the ages of 16 and 23 years may apply for citizenship only after eight years of permanent residence and six years of resident schooling (Grosch 1992:139). According to an article on Munich from the *Süddeutsche Zeitung* (9 June 1993), the number of people receiving German citizenship after the new foreigners law actually fell rather than rose, so that between March 1992 and February 1993 only 1,154 out of a total of 268,000 eligible foreigners assumed German citizenship, even though 78 percent fulfilled the necessary criteria.

For a number of foreigners, one problem with becoming a German citizen is the issue of preservation of identity. As Wolfgang Koydl points out, also in an article from the *Süddeutsche Zeitung* (7 June 1993), it should not be a question of having to relinquish one's non-German identity in order to become a German citizen, though the sentiment is clearly *Wer nicht ist wie wir, der hat kein Recht auf einen deutschen Pass* ("If you are not like us, you have no right to a German passport"). Rather, it ought to be possible to retain both identities—though many Germans and non-Germans seem to be at odds on the issue. Koydl states that "der Türke will sich als türkisches Mitglied in die deutsche Gesellschaft einfügen, der Deutsche erwartet, daß er seine türkische Identität abstreift."[7]

In "Wer ist Deutscher?"—another insightful article in the *Süddeutsche Zeitung* on German attitudes toward citizenship (4 February 1993)— Herbert Prantl points out how strong the echoes are of bygone days in the current debate on the naturalization of foreigners, which he calls a debate about *deutsches Blut und deutsche Art* ("German blood and German ways"). He explains that the issue goes back to *the Reichs- und Staatsangehörigkeitsgesetz* ("imperial and state nationality law"), which was passed in 1913 and which is based on *ius sanguinis*: "Deutscher ist nicht der, der in Deutschland geboren wird—nein, Deutscher ist nur der, der von Deutschen abstammt."[8] Further, he argues that this principle developed into a *Staatskult* ("national cult") during the Third Reich. Prantl understands why the extreme right would hang on to the principle of *ius sanguinis* and all that it implies, but does not see why the socialist factions would not wish to adopt the alternative *ius solis*. What is at stake here, it seems, is not simply immigrant identity, but Germans' own fears that by accepting foreigners and their children, as well as illegitimate children with a German parent, their own nationality, so sacred to the collective German psyche, would be compromised and even threatened with extinction.

That Germany needs clarity in its policies toward foreigners is certainly more crucial now than ever, since all indications are that the economy will continue to need foreign workers for the foreseeable future. Meier-Braun suggests that for the next twenty-five years Germany needs to import at least 300,000 immigrants each year to compensate for the steeply declining labor pool in the country (1992:225).[9] Moreover, he credits the foreign workers with Germany's sustained economic growth since 1985. According to the Institut der deutschen Wirtschaft in Cologne, without immigration the number of Germans under fifteen years of age will decrease from 13.7 million in 1990 to about 10 million in 2010. Indeed, the Institut suggests that to compensate for the decline in the 13–15 year old sector of the population, Germany's workforce needs at least 500,000 new foreigners per year. For the labor force as a whole (aged 15–65 years), the number of workers would fall by almost 4 million by the year 2010 without additional immigration. The decline in the native labor force is caused by a drop in the birthrate, which is even lower in eastern Germany than in the west, even in the face of changes in the abortion law, which have, in fact, led to staggering increases in the sterilization rate amongst young East German women (*German Tribune*, 12 June 1992).

Current demographic trends in general indicate that the German population of Germany will decrease by almost 20 million by the year 2030. Furthermore, the prospect of continued economic growth also adds to the need for further foreign labor. The German Economic Institute is adamant that all of the foreigners together—the Eastern Europeans, European Community members, and asylum seekers included—take nothing away from the German labor market, but rather fill crucial gaps in it that could otherwise only be compensated for (and are most unlikely to be compensated for) by an increase in the birthrate (Meier-Braun 1992:226).

Conclusion

What this chapter has shown is that there has never been one homogeneous group of foreigners, or even of foreign workers, in Germany, but rather that this population went or was called there for a variety of reasons and from a variety of places. In general, German policy toward foreign labor has always been to regard it as a temporary phenomenon, dependent on and responsive to the fluctuations of the national and world economy. Consequently, until relatively recently, neither the German government nor the German population as a whole has ever considered the possibility of integrating foreign workers and making them a permanent feature of German society. In particular, the German government has been reluctant to permit naturalization of foreign workers. This issue is still not solved.

One might laconically suggest, however, that the German government has been hoisted by its own classificatory petard, since treating foreigners uniformly as temporary residents has led to a number of social problems, which we will address in detail in the next chapter, where our principal focus will be on the issues of foreign-worker living conditions and education and the persistence of antiforeigner sentiment.

2. The Social Background

Introduction

Although there have been monumental problems between Germans and immigrants in recent years, and while one could not argue that German integration policies are particularly successful or even adequate at this point, nevertheless the past fifteen years have seen an appreciable improvement in social conditions for foreign workers in Germany, affecting almost every aspect of their daily lives. Some very troubling negative trends do persist, however, and contribute to racial tension within the country. German reunification in 1991 has also led to unique social problems which continue to take their toll both on the indigenous and the foreign population. In order to appreciate the scope of these changes in the social situation of foreign workers, we will first have to go back to the earlier years, when social conditions were particularly grim.

Once it was no longer compulsory for foreign workers to return to their country of origin after a fixed-term contract, it was inevitable they would remain in Germany for more extended periods. This development inevitably brought with it changes to the social system in Germany that had not been anticipated by the government, which had attended primarily to the short-term expedience, not to the long-term consequences, of the importation of foreign labor (*Rückblick* 1986:21).

Up until the 1980s, social policy and social conditions had conspired to make the "Gastarbeiter" what the 1987 edition of the almanac *Tatsachen über Deutschland* described as the largest "social minority," the largest "underprivileged sector," and a "fringe group." They comprised about 5.7 million people[1] out of a total population of 61.1 million.[2] In other words, foreign workers constituted at that time 7.5 percent of the total population of West Germany and a full 10 percent of its workforce.[3]

All through the 1970s and into the 1980s, very many foreign workers lived in sorely inadequate housing, some in ghetto-like ethnic enclaves in large cities. In general, they and their children suffered a number of disadvantages and deprivations, either caused by their lack of general education, illiteracy, and inability to communicate on an adequate level in German or clearly attributable to inadequate social provision by the German government.

The majority of foreign workers come from extremely poor, conservative, rural areas in their home country, and they suffer from severe culture shock upon moving to German cities. They find it very hard to adjust to the new way of life and daily customs of Germany, and help with integration has hitherto been less than forthcoming in the majority of cases.

Living Conditions

Living conditions for many foreign workers in Germany were, until fairly recently, notoriously bad. Herbert (1990:220) suggests that "[as] a whole . . . the living conditions of foreign workers remained the most externally visible sign of their underprivileged and disadvantaged situation in the Federal Republic well into the late 1970s."

Castles and Kosack point out that unconverted or inadequately converted attics in big blocks of flats constituted typical housing for foreign workers in Germany (1985:268). Herbert suggests that, since there were fixed agreements on wages and social benefits that (at least theoretically) put the foreigners on an equal footing with the Germans, housing was one of the areas in which employers (as well as many private landlords) could cut costs. Indeed, believing they were in Germany only temporarily, many of the foreigners themselves were not always averse to saving money by living for the short-term in undesirable conditions. Moreover, the majority of them were comparing conditions in Germany with those in their own countries, and were therefore more ready to regard the housing offered to them as reasonable (Herbert 1990:217–22). Foreign workers felt compelled on several levels to accept such housing:

> Because most guest workers entered West Germany with the prime intention of accumulating capital, and for various reasons remain uncertain about their length of stay, they tend to look for housing which satisfies their basic needs as cheaply as possible. Apart from the company dormitories, this is mostly found in the inner cities, within which their residential search is often conditioned by a desire to maintain proximity with their compatriots. Spatial proximity presents the opportunity of replicating some of the ambiance of their homeland, not only though patronage of local shops and cafés, but also through the use of the mother tongue. It also forms something of a defense against the low degree of social acceptance which they experience from the host popu-

lation. Indeed, many immigrants are introduced to these areas by personal contacts. Although homogenous enclaves of any great extent have not developed, the heterogenous ethnic composition of the guest workers adds an exotic vitality to certain sectors of the larger cities, which otherwise would undoubtedly be declining in population.

(Jones 1983:97)

It was, and still is, frequently the case that Germans and foreigners mix like oil and water in housing complexes. Even though they may both live in the same building, this does not necessarily guarantee contact. This situation has very often led to tensions between Germans and foreign workers. Jones (1983:94) discusses the sacrosanct nature of the entrance hall in German apartment houses. He suggests that while ethnic mixing may go on at other levels, the strict code of conduct that applies to shared hallways in apartment houses (vis-à-vis greetings, noise, cleanliness, smells, etc.) renders this the level at which true segregation occurs. Segregation can be by building or by floor, and research has shown that while whole apartment houses can be 100 percent of one ethnicity or another, whole floors within apartment houses are often this way.

Foreign workers have now lived in Germany for on average two decades, as we have seen, and they no longer live in the collective housing they had to take when they were first recruited. In particular, the number of foreigners living in slums has decreased markedly since 1984. In 1993 84 percent lived in rental apartments, while only 6.4 percent of foreign workers had managed to buy a home in Germany. Although it is impossible to know how much property foreign workers own abroad, we do know that the amount of money being transferred abroad has dropped to only 1,000 DM per capita per annum, which is about a third of the rate of transfer in 1970 (Thränhardt 1995:8–9).

By 1991 the accommodation of foreign residents in Germany was usually of normal standard, with kitchen, cellar, hot water, WC, bathroom, and telephone. Three-quarters of the apartments had central heating, though only 41 percent had a balcony or terrace and only 14 percent had a garden. Living space was also comparable with that of the native Germans per household, though per capita it was much lower than that of the Germans, because of the larger family size among foreigners.

While these improvements in conditions for foreigners are encouraging, they do need to be put into perspective. Although since reunification it has been very difficult indeed for a foreigner (or a native

German) to get a new apartment, this was not the case in the 1980s, on account of a building boom that resulted in many buildings standing empty, rendering them easier for foreigners to obtain. Moreover, once one has acquired an apartment in Germany, renters' law guarantees a fairly stable situation (Thränhardt 1995). While these improvements are encouraging, we need to stress that living in the same house or housing area as Germans is by no means the same thing as integration.

Household Structure and Income

There is a variety of household types amongst foreign population, just as there is amongst the indigenous Germans. The majority (44.2 percent) are households with children (compared with 38.6 percent of German households), and while most Germans live in one-person households, most foreigners live in families of four or more.

In 1991 the individual net income for foreigners was 377 DM per month less than that for Germans, though this was a marked improvement on the salary levels of the mid-eighties. While the average rent is still lower than that of indigenous Germans, it is rising faster, no doubt on account of demands for better quality and conditions. On the other hand, 29 percent of foreign households have to pay more than 30 percent of their expendable income on rent, and a further 19 percent have to pay more than 25 percent. However, it must be noted that foreigners earn the same as Germans within the same occupations, whether technical or unskilled. Salaried indigenous workers in white-collar positions earn 385 DM more than similarly employed foreigners, but this again is due to structural factors, in particular to the presence of a greater number of Germans in executive positions.

Within the foreign population, however, a woman's salary is much lower than a man's; moreover, women's earnings have fallen from 61.8 percent to 52.5 percent of men's since 1984. The structural reasons for this are the lower educational and training level of foreign women and their underrepresentation in salary negotiations.

The average household income for foreign families was 3,219 DM per month in 1993. Although households with more people generally bring in more wages overall, there is a sharp drop in the average income for households with more than four people. Given that most foreign households consist of four or more people, this means that on average they tend to be much worse off financially than indigenous Germans.

Education

As we have seen in Chapter 1, according to the German government, foreign workers were considered temporary guests, who were not supposed to stay in Germany for a long time. After the recruitment ban of 23 November 1973, many foreigners did return home (740,000 between 1973 and 1978), and the number of the foreign employed shrank from 2.6 million in 1973 to 1.6 million in 1985. But spouses and minor children continued to immigrate. The recruitment ban failed as an instrument of constraint particularly with the Turks: "Aus Gastarbeitern wurden Dauergäste und schließlich Einwanderer"[4] (Herrmann 1995:24).

This development had important consequences for the developmental prospects of many foreigners, especially with respect to education because many reunited family members were of school age. Schooling had already been declared compulsory for the children of foreigners in 1964. Between 1975 and 1980 the number of foreign schoolchildren rose by almost 50,000 per year, the majority of them being in either the *Grundschule* or the *Hauptschule*.

Integration into schools has been complicated by the patterns of movement among the dependents of foreign workers. This is particularly the case for the so-called *Seiteneinsteiger* ("late-comers," literally "side-entrants") and the *Pendelkinder* ("commuter children"). These two groups in particular did not have adequate command of German, and their socialization in the home country interfered with the new patterns of socialization in Germany. In general it has been the case that the older the children were on immigrating, the greater their problems have been in asserting their social identity and progressing in school.

The Seiteneinsteiger consist primarily of young Turkish children. Some had already completed their schooling in Turkey, though this was usually at the most five years of basic education. The problem of adjustment has been particularly acute for children who entered the German system very late. "Sie wurden dem mit der Übersiedlung verbundenen Kulturschock in der Pubertät ausgesetzt, besaßen nur eine für unsere Gesellschaft unzureichende Schulbildung, hatten keinen Beruf erlernt und sprachen kein Wort Deutsch"[5] (Herrmann 1995:24). These are the children who usually end up either as a life-long manual laborer or, worse, a long-term unemployment statistic in the Federal Republic.

While the Seiteneinsteiger often arrive in Germany too late to take advantage of the education system, the Pendelkinder commute back and forth between their nuclear family in Germany and their extended family in Turkey, allowing their parents to remain in Germany and work. Even when they have finished their schooling in Turkey, they are required to go to school again when they return to Germany (usually just before their sixteenth birthday, when they would lose their residency eligibility). A number of model projects have been carried out both at the national and local level and in the private sector to develop programs to promote the needs of foreign children in the German school system. Many other programs have been developed that address the specific deficits of these children as well as their socialization experiences.

On the whole, German educators have been at pains to react to the special needs of foreign children in their schools. There have been countless plans for cross-cultural and intercultural education projects, and bilingual schooling is also available in some states.[6]

Despite these efforts, the educational failure rate amongst all foreign children has remained stubbornly high. A great proportion of them still leave the *Hauptschule* without any qualifications. In 1983, when statistics were compiled for the first time, officially 40.7 percent failed, and estimates for the previous years are about 60 percent.[7]

The problems in schools and education begin for the children of foreign workers at the earliest stages. While 61.6 percent of German children are placed in kindergarten, only 48.6 percent of the foreign children are so provided for. The difference lies partly in the fact that there are local discrepancies in the provision of kindergarten places, but it is also the case that many of the kindergartens are linked to churches and religious organizations and are reluctant to give places to children of other religions, a relevance that affects the children of Turkish families in particular (Thränhardt 1995:10).[8]

But there is a noticeable improvement in the number of educational qualifications in the foreign population. While in 1983 only 3,299 foreign children gained the *Abitur*, in 1993 the number had increased to 11,376. The number of these children without a general school leaver's certificate (*Hauptschulabschluß*) has also dropped, though the contrast with mainstream German children is still great. Differences are particularly striking amongst the individual federal states. For example, while in North Rhine-Westphalia 52.6 percent of foreign children gained a school leaver's certificate, in Baden-Württemberg it was only 33.2 percent and in Bavaria, 25.2 percent. Different educational concepts and policies in the individual school systems are responsible for these discrepancies. For example, North Rhine-Westphalia enjoys an educational system in which it is particularly easy to move around between different types of school, whereas Bavaria still insists on segregated *Nationalklassen*, which do not particularly facilitate the attainment of educational qualifications (Thränhardt 1995:10).

There are other causes of the failure of foreign schoolchildren in the educational system that are not created in the school, but in the home, such as cramped living conditions, burdening the children with too many household and childcare responsibilities, and, of course, the inability of parents to help with schoolwork because of their own linguistic and educational deficiencies (Herrmann 1995:25). Hegele and Pommerin summarize the typical problems of foreign schoolchildren as follows (though they also recognize that the particular circumstances and difficulties of each child are different):

- appalling living conditions
- authoritarian style adopted by parents
- conflict amongst siblings
- parents' own lack of belonging, which is passed on to the children
- fear and competitiveness between foreign and German schoolchildren
- lack of employment prospects
- overextended and uncomprehending teachers
- lack of interest by the rest of society in the culture of the foreign children
- disturbing contacts with extremist groups from the home country when the children try to maintain their own culture
- feeling of not being understood or accepted anywhere, of not being allowed to develop one's own life, of constantly having to be on the defensive

(adapted from Hegele and Pommerin 1983:13–14)

The list of problems for foreign children has not grown much shorter since the mid-eighties, though of course the linguistic abilities of second and subsequent generations are generally improving.

Even once foreign children have left school, possession of paper qualifications does not guarantee the opportunity for professional training. Government positions are closed to foreigners, as are a number of jobs in the churches and church-run social services and organizations. In general, the number of foreign youths in apprenticeships and professional training courses is particularly low, though the numbers are growing (49,175 in 1984, compared with 119,849 in 1992). However, foreign students now also have to compete with Germans from the former GDR for the spaces available. Participation in such courses is clearly dependent upon structural factors, such as how many places are actually provided by the government, but social factors also figure largely in this issue. For example, Moslem girls are often prevented from pursuing vocational training by their parents. The Bundesinstitut für Berufsbildung, the Federal Institute of Occupational Training, found a correlation between foreign youths' participation in training courses and the following factors:

- age on entry into Germany
- parental home
- plans for remigration
- school attendance
- voluntary refusal of occupational training
- careers advising and careers information
- plans after leaving school

(adapted from Herrmann 1995:28)

The type of employment that a foreign youth aims for is also conditioned by family attitudes and the family's relative status in the home country. Particularly high social status accrues to white-collar positions and to the self-employed.

The lack of educational qualifications and opportunities for training, for whatever reasons, means that the second and third generations are forced, like the first-generation immigrants, to take on unskilled and semiskilled jobs. This is exactly what leads to the cycle of poverty and the general lack of social mobility among the foreign workers, as the figures on their participation in particular occupations across generations attest (see Table 2). Unemployment is particularly high amongst foreign youths in the 20–25 and 25–30 age groups, where we now find the former "side-entrants," and this problem is one that has yet to be addressed by the authorities (Herrmann 1995:25).

Employment Opportunities

Since first-generation foreign workers are often poorly educated or completely uneducated, they must consequently accept the more menial and unglamorous jobs that the Germans themselves are reluctant to do. A number of branches of industry are extremely dependent on foreign workers as their main source of labor. For example, these workers make up 35 percent of the wage earners in the automobile industry alone, and across all industries, over 50 percent of all shiftworkers. They are largely responsible for refuse disposal in many cities, and foreign women are by far the largest providers of commercial and domestic cleaning services (Bundesministerium 1989a 1:10). In general foreign workers make up a larger proportion of the workforce relative to their group size than their German compatriots—almost 80 percent of foreign women work, for example—though the financial compensation they receive is much lower than for the average German, owing to the type of work. Of all the foreign females employed in Germany, 35 percent are unskilled, 35 percent are semiskilled, and only 9.6 percent work in the professions. Lichtenberger suggests that foreign workers are necessary, in times of a surfeit of employment, to do five main types of work that the indigenous population is unwilling to undertake:

- jobs involving physical risk and exertion (e.g., heavy industry)
- open-air jobs subject to weather conditions (e.g., building industry)
- dirty jobs (e.g., industrial and domestic cleaning)
- jobs without clearly defined hours and without guaranteed free time (e.g., the hospitality trade, hotels, and catering)
- poorly paid jobs

(adapted from Lichtenberger 1984:78)

Castles and Kosack make clear the interrelatedness of seemingly independent factors that shape individual portions of foreign workers' lives. Specifically, they emphasize the importance of work type:

> The type of work available to immigrants does not merely govern their incomes. It also helps to determine what areas the immigrants settle in, how they interact with the indigenous labor force and population, and their social status. If immigrants are granted access only to a limited range of occupations on arrival, this causes concentration in certain towns and regions. Low incomes ensure that immigrants get the worst housing in run-down neighborhoods. Bad social conditions, therefore, result from the immigrants' initial subordinate position on the labor market. In turn, social deprivation hinders vocational advancement: high mobility in search of better housing and poor health due to insanitary conditions are factors which prevent promotion. Moreover, the areas in which immigrants are forced to settle by their low incomes tend to be those with overstrained and inadequate educational facilities. The children of immigrants are thus also at a disadvantage, and are likely to become manual workers like their fathers.
>
> (1985:57)

By 1992 the average foreign worker had kept his job for over 8.1 years, and belonged to the core personnel in industrial concerns (Thränhardt 1995:5). Table 2 provides a breakdown of employment figures across economic sectors. Since the early days of recruitment, foreigners have

Table 2. Total Employed and Number of
Foreign Workers in Selected Branches, 1993

Economic Sector	Total Employed N	%	Foreigners N	%
Agriculture, forestry	219,000	0.9	28,000	1.3
Manufacturing	8,105,200	35.1	945,200	43.3
Building	1,589,900	6.9	211,500	9.7
Services	5,307,700	23.0	547,300	25.1
Power, water, mining	417,300	14.3	28,200	1.3
Trade	3,307,900	1.8	214,900	9.8
Traffic, communications	1,179,900	5.1	101,300	4.6
Financial institutions, insurance	964,400	4.2	21,500	1.0
Non-profit organizations, private households	567,500	2.5	30,200	1.4
Regional corporations, social security	1,463,200	6.3	55,300	2.5
Total	23,122,000	100	2,183,400	100

Source: *Statistisches Jahrbuch für die Bundesrepublik Deutschland 1994*, Wiesbaden 1994 (adapted from Thränhardt, 1995:6)

worked primarily in the manufacturing industry, as well as in construction and mining, and this trend continues. They have not followed the national trend of increased participation in the service sector, and foreigners are most underrepresented in the civil service, banking, insurance, inland revenue, and accounting. Foreigners also have much less chance of promotion in their jobs; in fact, they are often in the most precarious positions. Consequently, a number of foreigners have striven to become self-employed. Italians and Greeks constitute the largest group of self-employed, with 9 and 14 percent respectively. Workers from Spain and the former Yugoslavia are more likely than those from other nations to be specialist workers. Yet, barely a quarter of all foreign residents are white-collar workers. Table 3 provides a breakdown of the occupational status of foreign workers.

Since the oil crisis of 1974, the proportion of unemployed foreigners in Germany has been higher than that of unemployed Germans, and in the past few years the rate has almost doubled, particularly amongst Turks, Italians, and Greeks. This is partly to do with their lower level of training and education, but it is also partly due to the fact that the jobs for which they were recruited are susceptible to market forces. There are few foreign workers in government, banking, welfare, and

Table 3. Occupational Status of Foreign Workers, by Country of Origin, 1993

Occupational status	Turkey (%)	Former Yugoslavia (%)	Italy (%)	Spain (%)	Greece (%)
Unskilled worker	15	13	15	16	14
Semiskilled worker	35	29	26	25	25
White-collar worker	17	23	24	23	23
Specialist/trades	25	32	26	30	24
Self-employed	6	3	9	7	14

Source: Translated from Thränhardt 1995:7

insurance positions. And prospects for improvement are not encouraging, owing to the fact that foreigners, in particular foreign women, are underrepresented in apprenticeships and job and professional training schemes (Thränhardt 1995:7).

The prospects are not all bad, however, and there are clear indications of improvements (however slow) in occupational status for foreign youth. While almost half of the first generation is employed in production industry, better linguistic abilities and higher educational qualifications are leading to an occupational shift in the younger generations. There also remains a difference in these generations between young men and women. In the 15–19 age group 45 percent and in the 20–24 age group 40.4 percent of men are employed in manufacturing. Amongst women, however, only 15.6 percent of the 15–19 age group and 24.2 percent of the 20–24 age group work in production; instead, the service sector dominates (54 percent and 46.7 percent, respectively) with commerce a close second (21.1 percent and 17.9 percent) (Herrmann 1995:28).

Ausländerfeindlichkeit

As we remarked in Chapter 1, the employment of foreign laborers in Germany has been fraught with social tension since at least the beginning of the century. The ethnic Poles who came to settle in the late 1800s encountered resentment and antipathy from native Germans, and the trend has persisted. Germany is like every other European country in this regard: Great Britain, France, Switzerland, Sweden, among others, all experience tensions and, indeed, sometimes extreme and violent racism. Of course, the major difference between Germany and the other

European countries is the execrable legacy of the Third Reich and the burden of guilt that remains.[8] Herbert (1990:198–99) argues that there is a "key nexus" between earlier and later groups of alien workers in Germany, whether they be the Fremdarbeiter of the German Reich or the postwar Ostvertriebene and refugees or the Gastarbeiter who migrated to Germany from the fifties onward. He argues that there is definite continuity in the West Germans' defensive reactions to the influx of these workers and that, indeed, in some areas (for example, East Prussia) the different groups might have been regarded by the locals simply as replacements for each other. This reaction might have been reinforced, Herbert argues, by the fact that in many towns and villages old military barracks have served as homes for a succession of outside workers, including National Labor Service (*Reichsarbeitsdienst*) work groups in the 1930s, Fremdarbeiter during World War II, displaced persons (frequently Jewish), expellees from the East, and Gastarbeiter from the 1950s onward (and we must now add refugees from Eastern Europe, the Middle East, and Africa in the 1990s). Herbert suggests that it was the scale of the influx of aliens itself that caused the tension, though occasionally there was also stiff competition between foreigners and locals on the labor market. He contends that the relatively disadvantaged position of the Vertriebene contributed directly toward the development of the two-tier labor market system and to the general process of *Unterschichtung* (199).

While important differences distinguished the Vertriebene from the Gastarbeiter (such as the impossibility of the Vertriebene returning home, their right to vote, their social heterogeneity, and, not least significantly, their ability to speak German and consequently to integrate more easily), there are persistent similarities between the two groups that have forged a direct link between past and present German social and economic responses to these groups (198–201).

By the mid-sixties *Ausländerfeindlichkeit* had reared its ugly head in Germany again, as Herbert observes: the *Rheinischer Merkur*, a radical conservative daily newspaper, was criticizing West Germans "who find it 'generous of us' to allow the 'dagos' (elsewhere they're called 'spaghetti eaters') to work in the Federal Republic" and "signs on restaurants proclaiming *Proibizione per Italianos* (in incorrect Italian)" (225). On the whole, however, such extreme remarks were countered by general pronouncements about the usefulness and positive economic effects of employing foreign labor in Germany. Herbert cites the following article from the *Hamburger Echo* in 1962, which makes a plea for tact and tolerance:

The relations between guest workers and the Germans in general, and their German fellow workers in particular, are anything but harmonious. By application of patience and understanding, the difference in mentality can . . . be eliminated as a factor aggravating the climate on the job. The guest worker is not some sort of "strange animal," who gesticulates and talks in a loud voice. Likewise, he is not any mere appendage to a machine. In "national" terms, every people has its advantages and disadvantages. The fact that some people would appear to have a more advantageous position than others due to economic and technological development certainly does not mean that there are first- and second-class peoples. . . . Another aspect to bear in mind is that these hundreds of thousands of guest workers are the object of a successful form of development aid—successful because of its effectiveness in terms of human relationships. And specifically when it comes to these relationships between human beings, the hosts should never forget that, in the course of history, guests have often proven quite useful for their hosts—and vice versa! If these guests have positive experiences during their stay in the Federal Republic, later on they will be Germany's best ambassadors back home in their own countries.

(226)

There was essentially relatively little unrest about foreign workers in Germany until the recession of 1966–67, at which time foreigners and unemployed Germans were directly competing for employment. As a number of commentators have stressed (for example, Herbert 1990:228), Germans felt then, as they had felt all along, that the foreign workers were in Germany temporarily and that they should be sent home in times of economic strain. Since the recession was quickly over, interracial tensions did not increase to any great extent, and, in fact, the recruitment and expansion of foreign labor continued in the post-recession period. It was once again felt, as *Industriekurier* observed in 1968, that "the return on foreign labor considerably exceeds investment costs" (cited in Herbert 1990:229).

Castles and Kosack (1985:433–34) discuss a survey by the Institut für Angewandte Sozialwissenschaft, the Institute for Applied Social Science (INFAS), in 1966 which concluded: "On the whole one can say that the Germans are not particularly ready to put up with or favor the employment of foreign workers. About two-thirds of the population would like to get rid of these employees." Indeed, the INFAS report states that 40 percent of skilled workers and 60 percent of semiskilled and unskilled workers wanted to get rid of foreign workers altogether. Workers particularly, though not exclusively, believed that foreigners posed an economic threat to Germany, and a number of them believed foreigners to be a threat to their own jobs. The INFAS survey also showed that German workers had a number of negative, preconceived opinions of foreigners, including that they chase German women and girls, they start fights, they strain the social services, and they spread communism. Some also remained of the opinion that foreigners were undesirable because of the mixing of races through intermarriage. Other independent surveys made at the same time confirmed the results of the INFAS survey and added complaints about the foreign workers' stupidity, vulgarity, and objectionable behavior. Castles and Kosack also point to evidence of a definite class-based split in attitudes toward foreigners: the working class is much more likely to perceive them negatively than the professional class, who would appear to understand the economic necessity for foreign labor (1985: 434). Not surprisingly, then, the professional-class population is more open to engaging in social relations with foreigners than the working-class population, though opportunities for such relations are clearly limited, since work, educational levels, income, and living conditions, among other things, confine foreign workers to working-class interaction. "It is frequently implied that prejudice is the main determinant of the subordinate position and bad conditions of immigrants, and that these can be changed by educational campaigns designed to change attitudes. In reality, the relationship between discrimination and prejudice is a dialectical one: discrimination is based on economic and social interests and prejudice originates as an instrument to defend such discrimination. In turn, prejudice becomes entrenched and helps to cause further discrimination" (430). Essentially, a simple formula can explain the incidence of prejudice: the more directly threatened people feel by foreigners, in terms of employment, social prospects, competition for housing, social benefits, etc., the more likely they are to experience direct feelings of prejudice and hostility against the foreign population.

There is no disputing the fact that such feelings of prejudice have been, and continue to be, strengthened and exploited by political movements in Germany—as they have been and still are throughout the rest of Western Europe. The Nationaldemokratische Partei Deutschlands, the National Democratic Party of Germany (NPD), and the newer right-wing political group the Republikaner, have persistently used opposition to foreigners as one of the strongest planks of their respective political platforms. In the late 1980s and into the 1990s, support for the

Republikaner and other right-wing extremist movements has grown. This has been stimulated particularly by reunification, since workers from the eastern part of Germany have also felt themselves to be in direct and fierce competition with non-Germans for jobs, housing, social benefits, and social contacts.

The problems have been exacerbated by the huge influx of refugees and asylum seekers, who have come to Germany on account of its very liberal asylum policy. As we have observed several times already, whenever there was a visibly large influx of foreigners to Germany, racial tension grew. Not suprisingly, this pattern persisted in 1992, when the number of refugees and asylum seekers entering Germany reached a staggering 438,000 (Aktion Gemeinsinn 1993). In that year there were 2,300 attacks on foreigners in Germany, including acts of arson and murder, in which seventeen people lost their lives. The new wave of violence began in the autumn of 1991 with the attack on an asylum seeker's residence in Hoyerswerda. This was followed by the attack in Rostock-Lichtenhagen. Since both these attacks took place in the new federal states, they created the impression that the East was particularly susceptible to such outbursts of aggression. In fact, xenophobic acts in the west of Germany are equally severe, as proved in the most terrible fashion by the murder of a Turkish foreign worker and two children in Mölln. However, it is generally the case, throughout unified Germany, that large cities display greater tolerance than smaller towns and villages (Bade 1994:189).

While memories of the violence stay with us, we must not forget the vast opposition to it shown by German citizens, manifested in huge candlelight processions and vigils in Berlin, Cologne, Dresden, Hamburg, Hannover, Munich, Stuttgart—to name but some of the cities. There are also hundreds of church and civic campaigns (*Bürgerinitiative*) and aid programs aimed at reducing tensions and facilitating integration.

But the list of incidents is long, and attacks are clearly not aimed just at refugees and asylum seekers, but also at long-term foreign-worker residents. Slogans such as *Deutschland den Deutschen* ("Germany for the Germans") and *Ausländer 'raus* ("foreigners out"), though rejected by 89 percent of Germans, crop up everywhere, and there is no doubt that dark-skinned foreigners and Moslems are the hardest hit by the xenophobia. On the whole, however, the problems in Germany are no worse than in, say, France or Great Britain. It is to be hoped that improvements in conditions for Germans and improvements in the legal situation of foreign residents, as detailed in Chapter 1, will reduce racial tensions in the future, though the potential for racist expression will remain and continue to call for vigilance on the part of the government and the ordinary citizens and residents of Germany.

Conclusion

In this chapter I have attempted to give a brief summary of the social conditions and issues facing foreigners in Germany. I have tried to put a positive face on the question and to document that the social conditions in which the foreign workers live have improved considerably since the fifties. There is no doubt that enormous problems remain: problems of integration, education, social equality, and racial tension; however, on the whole, the problems of foreign workers have changed since their beginnings as guests in Germany because they have become recognized as de facto immigrants to the country. Later, in Chapter 4, we will see how the immigrant literary community has mirrored this evolution in its own development, and that, as in real life, where foreign workers were once content to be on the outside of German society, they are now knocking on the door of the mainstream and asking to be let in.

A central problem facing all immigrants to a new country is the lack of language. Many of the problems we have discussed in this chapter would be alleviated if the immigrants to Germany had better linguistic skills. In the following chapter we will take a close look at the linguistic development of immigrants in light of the issues already presented, in order to demonstrate the inextricable interconnectedness of language, society, history, and cultural identity.

3. From *Pidgindeutsch* to Standard German: The Linguistic Situation

Introduction

Since the late 1960s there has been much discussion in applied linguistics and sociolinguistics about the nature and function of the German that is spoken by foreign workers in Germany—to such an extent that a new subfield of linguistics, *Gastarbeiterlinguistik*, developed. Following the trends in other areas of linguistics, the first studies aimed to discover the universal characteristics and strategies involved in the acquisition of German by foreigners. A central theme of this research was the varietal status of foreigner German: is it a pidgin, a creole, or just another learner dialect? As we will see in this chapter, researchers have differed greatly in their conclusions on the subject, partly as a result of the inconclusive and often competing definitions of such varieties as pidgin, creole, interlanguage, and xenolect to be found in the literature.

However, almost all of the studies of "Gastarbeiterdeutsch" (for that is what most researchers called it) ignored or failed to convey clearly enough, until relatively recently, that different varieties of Foreign Worker German naturally *coexist* in Germany and that progression toward Standard German (or, for that matter, fossilization at a lower stage of acquisition) cannot be taken for granted, but is conditioned for each individual by social, demographic, and environmental factors.

As the pendulum swung away from viewing immigrants collectively toward viewing them as individuals, later studies of the German of foreign workers in Germany began to concentrate less on matters of form and definition and more on the dimensions of interpersonal contact involved in conversation with nonnative speakers of German. Such studies have been informed by work in social psychology on accommodation theory and by pragmatics and discourse analysis. In this chapter we will also briefly consider this more communication-oriented approach.

Yet perhaps the two most interesting questions we must address here concern the symbolic function of Foreign Worker German and the role of the subfield Gastarbeiterlinguistik itself. Gastarbeiterlinguistik has received criticism on two main counts, both of which seem to constitute reasonable objections: first, that it originally focused on universal structural characteristics and neglected the human and interpersonal aspects of language acquisition, even in the face of the serious social difficulties evident among foreign workers; and second, that by naming the variety *Pidgindeutsch* and insisting on the field of Gastarbeiterlinguistik, while neglecting individual and group variation, linguists have inadvertently *caused* (I would say *contributed to*) the ethnicization of the Gastarbeiter as a whole. These issues testify once again to the power of language and to the central role of categorization struggles in the quest for status in society. We shall discuss these two issues and their theoretical underpinnings below.

Structural Features of Foreign Worker German

In the late 1960s German linguists suggested that the spontaneously acquired German of first-generation adult immigrants had much in common with contact languages found elsewhere in the world. Michael Clyne (1968) first introduced the notion of Pidgindeutsch, and soon projects developed at major universities (for example, Heidelberg, Free University-Berlin, Wuppertal, Stuttgart, and Konstanz) to investigate the linguistic behavior of immigrants in the Federal Republic. The Heidelberger Forschungsprojekt Pidgindeutsch set the agenda for the first phase of research, whose priorities were, first, to determine the structural peculiarities of Foreign Worker German and, second, to determine the social circumstances that led to its development.

The Heidelberg project defined Pidgindeutsch essentially as a social-group variety of German, restricted in both function and social domain, that evinces a degree of formal simplification caused at least in part by the social and communicative isolation of its speakers. This simplified variety of German usually remains "frozen" (or fossilized) at a particular level of linguistic competence, which means that a large number of immigrants fail to progress toward the local standard. Structurally, Pidgindeutsch is preliminarily characterized as having minimal or no morphology, a markedly reduced inventory of grammatical categories in comparison with Standard German, a limited lexicon, and idiosyncratic word order patterns (Heidelberger Forschungsprojekt 1975:83).

Bodemann and Ostow concur that the German of foreign workers features "'grammatical leveling' on the one hand and general reduction in form on the other" (1975:135). Typical of the leveling or "universalization" that they detect are the "drastic" reduction of verbal inflections; the reduction of forms in the declension of adjectives, articles, and nouns; and the process of lexico-semantic extension, as well as significant influence of the first language (L1) on phonology. They also propose several general characteristics for Foreign Worker German[1]:

1. Foreign Worker German tends, independently of potential moods, to anchor the syntactic order as Subject-Verb-Object.
2. Foreign Worker German favors the proximity of an auxiliary to the main verb—for example, *aber er **wollte** nix **machen** neue Fabrik* (Standard German: *aber er wollte keine neue Fabrik machen* "but he did not want to make a new factory").
3. But Foreign Worker German puts negation before the main verb—for example, *ich **nix mache** Menschenskind* (Standard German: *ich mache nichts, Menschenskind* "I'm not doing anything, for goodness' sake"). Foreign Worker German also places the negator, when it is present, between the auxiliary and the main verb—for example, *aber er wollte **nix** machen neue Fabrik*; literally, "but he wanted not to make new factory" (Standard German: *aber er wollte keine neue Fabrik machen*).
4. Foreign Worker German does not separate separable verbal prefixes—for example, *jetzt diese ältere Leute **rausmachen*** (*Standard German: jetzt macht er diese älteren Leute 'raus*) "now he's putting these older people out."

Bodemann and Ostow emphasize throughout that this simplified code is characterized by regular and systematic structures, rather than being haphazard, ad hoc, or simply "broken" German (1975:135–37). Hinnenkamp proposes the following characteristic types of simplification:

1. loss of pre- and postpositions
2. loss of nominal inflection and agreement
3. deletion of the copula
4. generalization of the infinitive
5. change in word order
6. loss of overt question marking
7. external placement of propositional qualifiers
8. juxtaposition of subordinating clauses
9. lexical and grammatical multifunctionality
10. periphrasis

(1984:157)

In a very influential study, Jürgen Meisel (1975a) compares features of English, German, French, and Finnish foreigner talk with those of foreign workers' speech. Foreigner talk is a reduced form of language produced by native speakers to talk to nonnative speakers (similar to motherese or caretaker speech, used by competent speakers to learners of a language).[2] He suggests that these types of language use all display similar strategies of simplification. The following chart is my emended version of Meisel's description (1975a:35–46) of typical features of Foreign Worker German based on these simplification strategies:

1. Use of foreign words, not necessarily of the speakers' native language:
   amigo, capito, compris
   "friend," "understood," "understood"
2. Overgeneralization of Standard German words:
   viel dumm
   "much stupid"
   Ich nix mit kopf arbeit.
   "I not with head work"
   Niks gut wetter.
   "not good weather"
   Zwei monat nix arbeit!
   "two month not work"
3. *Du* for *Sie* (second person singular/intimate pronoun for second person plural/polite pronoun):
   Du viel arbeit!
   "you much work"
   Du verstehen was Frau sagt?
   "you understand what woman says?"
4. Analytical paraphrase of "complex" expressions:
   nix arbeit (arbeitslos)
   "not work" ("unemployed")
   mehr geld (Lohnerhöhung)
   "more money" ("pay rise")
   andere platz (anderswo)
   "other place" ("elsewhere")
   diese hand (links/rechts)
   "this hand" ("left/right")
   nix gut (schlecht)
   "not good" ("bad")
   tot machen (töten)
   "dead make" ("kill")
5. Decomposed predicates:
   Ganze Mafioso, mach kaputt drei Mensche.
   "complete mafioso, makes kaputt three people"
6. Missing elements:
   a. Articles, especially definite articles, typically within prepositional phrases and in subject-noun phrases:

Leuten gut, Geld gut, aber was machen mit Fuss?
"people good, money good, but what do with foot?"
Wir kommen aus Türkei.
"we come from Turkey"
(Standard German: *Wir kommen aus **der** Türkei.*)
b. Prepositions:
Ampel stehen bleiben.
"traffic light stand stay"
c. Copula, auxiliaries, and main verbs, most frequently the copula:
Nachher Griechenland.
"afterward Greece"
Kind alles in der Türkei geboren.
"child all in (the) Turkey born"
d. Personal pronouns, typically in subject position:
Zwei Monat nix arbeit.
"two month not work"
7. Inflectional endings on verbs, adjectives, and nouns are omitted:
Ich nix mit Kopf arbeit. Ich hier arbeit.
"I not with head work. I here work"
8. Pronouns in imperative:
Du bitte sprechen!
"you please speak"
9. Word order:
Milan hat gesagt sein Name.
"Milan has said his name"
(Standard German: *Milan hat seinen Namen gesagt.*)
Und dann hat gesehen E. Feuer auf Dach.
"and then has seen E. fire on roof"
"Then E. saw fire on the roof."
(Standard German: *Und dann hat E. Feuer auf dem Dach gesehen.*)
Im Momento ich möchte bleiben hier.
"at the moment I wish to stay here"
(Standard German: *Im Moment möchte ich hier bleiben.*)
10. Sentences containing an embedded clause are rare. If they do appear, complementizers and pronouns may be missing.

Meisel goes so far as to propose (in line with generativist thinking) that such strategies of simplification are universal and that second-language (L2) acquisition proceeds via these strategies, rather than by mere imitation. He crucially distinguishes between two types of simplification (and suggests that there might be more): "restrictive" simplification allows the speaker to use only already acquired grammar, while "elaborative" simplification prepares the speaker for the next step on the road to the L2.³ Restrictive simplification is used more often during earlier stages of L2 acquisition. Some speakers never abandon it and hence develop fossilized varieties of the L2, while those who progress toward successful acquisition of the L2 are more likely to make better use of elaborative simplification.

In a more recent analysis of the verb morphology of the German of adult foreign workers, Blackshire-Belay (1991:21, 25, 47, 51–52, 149–50, 204–6, 209) detects in her subjects processes of simplification similar to those found by Meisel:

1. Her informants used the infinitive as an unmarked form to represent all inflectional categories, for example: *nachher möchten mehr immer bleiben* ("afterwards want more always stay," that is, "afterward **he wanted** to stay there longer).⁴
2. Her informants frequently used structures that could possibly be interpreted as statal passives, but did not employ the target passive form with *werden*, for example: *es **war** damals richtig gemacht* "it was in those days right done" (Standard German: *es **wurde** damals richtig gemacht*).
3. Her informants used verbs unmarked for the present (or "nonpast")⁵ tense, sometimes accompanied by an adverbial marker to indicate time reference, for example: *1972 ich **kommen** [infinitive] in Deutschland* ("1972 I come to Germany").
4. Her informants used "nonpast" indicative forms to indicate past, for example: *weiß [present] nix genau erstemal wie geht mit arbeit* ("know not exactly first how goes with work," that is, "at first I didn't really know how it would go with work").
5. Her informants tended not to preserve grammatical distinctions in modality. None of the subjects in the study used the subjunctive.
6. Her informants were able to produce imperatives, albeit in what Blackshire-Belay describes as an "innovative form," so that the intonation, rather than the syntax, marks the meaning; thus, if they have question intonation, such constructions could also be interpreted as polite requests.
7. Her informants generated "admixtures" or "invented forms."
    a. Most of her informants used an innovative form of verb + second person indicative ending (-*st*) followed by the second person familiar pronoun (*du*) for imperatives, a construction not found in the target; for example, ***bringst du***

meine Lotto auch[6] ("bring you my Lotto too," that is, "bring me my Lotto ticket too").
  b. Most of her informants used novel combinations of auxiliary verb + another verb form not found in Standard German to represent a past construction, for example: *hat kommen* [infinitive] for Standard German *ist gekommen* and *hab arbeit* for Standard German *hab' gearbeitet.*
  c. Her informants often used modals in conjunction with nonstandard verbal forms, for example, with a verbal stem: *diese Grund war weil bin ich **mußte** in Deutschland **komm** so* ("this reason was because am I had to in Germany come so," that is, "this was the reason why I had to come to Germany in this way").
8. Her informants shared a number of features, but ranged in ability, with some closer to the superstrate language than others.

In other words, Blackshire-Belay's data show that there is a *continuum* of different facility in the target language, which is a point we will come back to subsequently in our discussion of a creole continuum.

To sum up all of the above findings on the structure of Foreign Worker German, then—regardless of what these researchers actually label this variety—it is characterized by regular and systematic differences from Standard German on all levels of language. Vocabulary is reduced, and paraphrase and lexicosemantic extension are salient features. On the morphological level, endings are simplified in both the noun phrase and the verb phrase. What is striking is that, rather than using a system of verbal morphemes to indicate tense, adverbials are relied on to convey time reference; that is, like many creoles and highly analytic standard languages such as Chinese and Vietnamese, Foreign Worker German indicates time relations lexically or pragmatically, rather than morphosyntactically. Word order is also very simple in comparison to Standard German, being relatively fixed; sentences containing embedded or subordinate clauses are also quite rare. The most significant feature of Foreign Worker German is simplification (if, indeed, one can talk about the simplification of a system that has not been fully acquired). It is exactly this notion of a simplified code that leads to the link with pidgin and creole studies, as we will see later in this chapter.

While the above studies regard simplification strategies as a major source of Foreign Worker German, other researchers, notably Meyer-Ingwersen (1975) and Gilbert (1983), look rather to the transfer or interference hypothesis for the source of differences between Foreign Worker German and Standard German, with Gilbert in particular linking this to pidginization. Nevertheless, most specialists (for example, Meisel 1983) now agree that, except in phonology and in culture-specific areas of the lexicon, straightforward transfer from the native language does not play a significant role in second-language acquisition, but rather that universal strategies of acquisition, such as simplification, are more essential factors.[7]

Varieties of Foreign Worker German

The majority of studies looked in the early stages for the common structural characteristics of Foreign Worker German across speakers, in line with general first and second-language acquisition studies that disregarded the individual in search of language universals. In the course of these investigations, however, no single, monolithic form of Foreign Worker German could be found; instead, many forms were found to coexist both at the same time and in the same communities—and even within the same family. For some speakers these forms indicate fossilization, while for others they represent a stage in a dynamic progression toward the native target.

In discussing his informants in the 1975 Heidelberger Forschungsprojekt Pidgindeutsch (HPD), for example, Dittmar noted the following two extremes of German on an overall continuum of varieties:

> (a) One, two or three word utterances (mostly nominal, pronominal or adjectival expressions in adverbial, subject or predicate function; small percentage of morphologically marked verbs) strongly influenced by elements of the native language and overlaid with the NL phonology.
>
> (b) The sentences of the advanced learner which display the average complexity of spoken German are clearly influenced by the local dialect variety (in this case, Palatine German) in phonology, morphology and lexicon, and, apart from the dialect-specific pleonastic use of relative and subordinating adjuncts[8] in dependent clauses, they display properties of spoken colloquial German.
>
> (Dittmar 1979:372–74)

In between these extremes, informants evinced a variety of interim forms differing primarily in terms of their relative lexical and syntactic complexity and displaying their own idiosyncratic rule systems that differ in nature both from the native language and the target language.

From Pidgindeutsch *to Standard German* 59

HPD (1975) proposed four general stages along the continuum of the migrants' development of German, which are summarized by Clyne (1984:91) as follows:

Phase 1: Deficient knowledge of German, better comprehension than production.

Phase 2: Contact with Germans and other guest workers, but they are not part of the main communication network and the subjects' German is insufficient for their communication needs.

Phase 3: Relatively stable; pidgin is integrated with their social and communicative needs; no motivation for further language acquisition.

Phase 4: Completely integrated; speech gravitates towards regional dialect.

Phases 1–3 are the most frequently encountered categories. It must be stated that these levels are not intended to be considered absolute or discrete, so that the number of phases is technically arbitrary. Rather, the phases meld into one another, on the one hand, and simultaneously display characteristics of other levels, on the other. (Moreover, this four-phase taxonomy could well be applied to scenarios for any L2 acquisition.)

In terms of syntax, the HPD subjects could be divided into four groups representing four phases of development, which I summarize here, adapting Dittmar's description and using his original examples.[9]

(1) At the lowest level sentences consist of unexpanded nominals or nominals preceded by a determiner. These utterances function as descriptive, generally temporal or locative elements. Sentences largely (though not completely) lack subject and verb (other than *ich* and *du*) and display no morphology.
EXAMPLE:
eh, wanne, wann isch edrink, trei uhe, trei uhe, ein man, e, eine mal deutsch, eh, ein gaste bieh alles, eh, wann isch drink, chef ekom, zage, "he! was mag du, uh,"... warum isch nix, warum eh, warum eh [Alfred] gome bieh, isch bezahl, warum isch nixs drink?[10]
TRANSLATION:
"Once when I wanted a drink, there is a German colleague who went for a case of beer around three o'clock in the afternoon, the boss came and he said, 'Hey! what are you doing, you there, huh?' Why shouldn't I have the right to drink?' "

(Dittmar 1979:138–39)

(2) Learners at this slightly higher level increasingly produce sentences containing subject and verb, and there is a limited amount of pronominalization. Nominals are more frequently expanded with articles. There is a limited number of attributive adjectives and complements accomaning nouns. Rudimentary attempts to use prepositional phrases and to mark verbs for time and mood are also observable. There are very few complex sentences, restricted to adverbial clauses.
EXAMPLE:
meine kinde viel tschimpfe zu mieh, viel tschimpfe uñ sagen tsag isch nie uñ uñ komme sohñ fumfe jahre kom iñ die schule un dam bisele sch eh lese schbani uñ andre, un dañ komme hieh, maestra foh die schule immeh schimfe "ho, deine soh viel dum, deine soh viel duñ"; un da eh schimfe, tsage "meine soh ni duñ. warum du nie spresche schbanik? schweh su dieh, a foh mein soh au schweh . . . lañsa, un da mein soh lerne."
TRANSLATION:
"My children often complain to me, they complain. My son went to school at the age of five. He learned to read Spanish, and other things besides. And then he came here. The schoolteacher is always complaining: 'Oh! how dumb your son is, your son is very dumb.' Then I get angry and I say: 'My son is not dumb! Why don't you speak Spanish yourself? It's difficult! Well, for my son it's German that is difficult! Not so fast, and my son will learn German too.' "

(3) The third phase is characterized largely as an expansion of phase two: pronominalization (though restricted to subjects) increases and nominal groups are differentiated by a wider use of articles, quantifiers and attributes. While still adverbial clauses, dependent clauses are better differentiated according to adverbial function. However, although the learner has a broader range of rules, certain of them show up remarkably frequently. Moreover, many of these structures still do not produce utterances that convey immediately transparent meaning.
EXAMPLE:
wann viel nix igal ei, eine stunde sweisse mache ode swei stund ode tage ode eine monat, mach nix, abe wann jente tage jente, des ima son le-eschecht machen, das son schlegt; de mask machen nix, wann jente tage, de de maske machen nix; ja, vielleicht sie jet kommen beiñ wohnezimme, ne? immer kanze f- ganze fabrik imme laufeñ, vleich eine freun da sweisse mache uñ andre so, ni lins un rechs, un die

andre gas immer au selber mache, wann se fort machen wie-wie seine plas arbeite un de maske muß raus machen die maske, ne?
TRANSLATION:
"When one has been a welder for a long time, it is not the same. It doesn't matter to do welding for an hour or two a day or a month, but when one does welding every day. Yes, when you go to the cloakroom, you have to go through the whole factory. And often there are fellows welding here and there, one on the right and one on the left, and the neighbor produces gases. And when you remove your mask, there are gases at the place where you are. And you have to remove the mask."

(4) The fourth level of acquisition is significantly more complex and varied than the phases of acquisition discussed so far. Rules generally reflect their syntactic and semantic function in the German target language (sufficient temporal and modal means are available to mark the verbs; the functions of adverbial and attributive determinants can be marked by appropriate surface markers, etc.); overloading of sentences with nominal groups is avoided by an increasing use of the pronominal system; while not completely nativelike, the case and verb morphology is in general used discriminatingly (especially in marking the finite and infinite verb forms, which serves to ensure comprehensibility); as well as various types of adverbial clause, nominal and attributive clauses are also formed, that is, the proportion of subordination per sentence increases appreciably; the varieties of the advanced learner are in general strongly colored by local dialect features.

EXAMPLE:
ik wah da wah ein donnerstag und hab ik am acht uhe . . . und dann hab ich zu ihre sohn gesach "ich möchte heute mittag um drei uhe zu maue—village mauer zum sahnahtz geh, isch abe große schmezen" un de sag "gut." so um sieben uhe bis acht uhe mohgens ab ik das gesach, ne? gut, also ik am alber drei feieraben machen, ne, so normal, ne aha, bei dem immer länger bleiben un nik bezahle überstunde, gar nix.
TRANSLATION:
"It was a Thursday. And then I said to his son at eight o'clock: 'Today, at three, I want to go to the dentist. The pain is very bad.' Then he said, 'all right!' It was between seven and eight o'clock in the morning when I said that. Fine. So I finished

work at 2:30, that is normal. But I often stayed longer, and that he didn't pay me for, not even the extra hours."

(Dittmar 1979:138–46)

The interim points in this acquisition sequence represent various stages of (generally diminishing) reduction of German, which correspond to different verbal strategies for conveying meaning. Dittmar maintains that this learning process is steered primarily by social factors, the most influential being contact with Germans in leisure time, contact with Germans at work, and age of arrival in Germany. Less important but still significant influencing factors are length of schooling and attained occupational qualification. Interestingly (and due no doubt to the rapid onset of fossilization in natural L2 acquisition), neither the length of stay nor the nationality or gender of an informant had any influence on the acquisitional process, particularly after the first six years (1979:198–209). The significance of social contact with Germans as a factor is therefore not to be underestimated. Indeed, even the type of accommodation in which the foreign worker lived was a significant environmental factor in the Heidelberger Forschungsprojekt Pidgindeutsch study, depending on whether it permitted contact with Germans or not. Dittmar points out that the workplace is clearly the most likely venue for communication with Germans, and this likelihood varies with the nature of the occupation (i.e., the greater the need for cooperation, the greater the need for communication), the type of workplace (i.e., levels of noise and of contact with Germans affect communication needs), and the position in the company (i.e., a foreman or interpreter must communicate more than a laborer). In general, however, the research shows that Germans and foreigners rarely communicate on any topic other than work and that the probability of social interaction increases only with promotion up the work hierarchy. A connection has also been perceived between social contact and age of entry into Germany. In the main, it appears to be the case that the younger a foreigner is on entry, the more likely he or she will be able to break down the barriers to communication. Finally, and not surprisingly, Dittmar perceives a strong correlation between educational level and language acquisition, claiming that it makes a big difference whether a worker has little schooling (0–2 years) or has completed a basic education, and whether a worker comes from an agricultural or an industrial background (377).[11]

That competing varieties of Foreign Worker German exist is corroborated by Blackshire-Belay's study. She divides her seventy-eight informants, who have all been in Germany over ten years, into the following two broad types:

Type 1
Limited contact with Germans, more contact with foreigners of different nationalities. Communication needs are met. There is no motivation at all for further language acquisition.

Type 2
More integrated into German society. Usage is more targetlike, but the individual is still recognizable as a member of the foreign worker community.

(1991:207)

Once again, contact with Germans is the trigger for the more advanced type (Type 2), which indeed is represented by very few of the speakers within the foreign worker community, on account of the general separation between Germans and foreign workers and constant interaction among the adult workers of different nationalities.

These findings accord with the work of Orlovic-Schwarzwald (1978) and Keim (1984), and it has been suggested that while, notionally at least, bilingual competence can be attained by older learners, the psychosocial barriers to successful acquisition are less likely to be present in younger speakers, and consequently younger learners tend to learn with greater facility.[12] Keim (1984) established other important social and psychosocial factors influencing the acquisition of German by the twelve adult Turkish workers in her study. Successful acquisition correlated with the intention to stay in Germany for a long time, a critical but reserved attitude toward Turkish political and religious practices, and an understanding of the legal position of a foreigner working in Germany.

To summarize, the first major findings of Foreign Worker German projects show that we are dealing, structurally speaking, with a code or set of codes that are highly simplified (relative to the standard in the target language) and quite variable across speakers. Foreign Worker German comprises variable and simplified forms of German that have the potential to develop in the direction of the regional standard, but that are often arrested at a lower level of competence on account of social factors—on account, in particular, of restricted contact with German native speakers.

These structural systems are broadly consistent across speakers, and they do not always resemble either the native language or standard (or colloquial) German. Bodemann and Ostow make this point about their Stuttgart informants: "Auch hier ist festzuhalten, daß die vom Fremdarbeiter gewählte Form weder dem Schwäbischen noch dem umgangssprachlichen Deutschen entspricht"[13] (1975:140). Dittmar maintains that the interim systems of German that learners have acquired are "relatively separate from those of the source language, simplified in essential characteristics in comparison with the target variety (pidginized) and independently productive as learner systems" (1979:377). Again, however, it is worth pointing out that the systems that have been ascertained are usually *interim* systems, that is, they represent "freeze-frame" points on a continuum of varieties, from highly reduced and idiosyncratic forms to highly consistent and nativelike systems.

Is *Pidgindeutsch* a Pidgin?

Most researchers on pidgin and creole languages would acknowledge the existence of pidgins in noncolonial contexts, such as in trading situations (for example, Russenorsk or Chinook Jargon). However, while there has been general agreement about its structural characteristics, its strategies of simplification, and its overall development, the classification of Foreign Worker German as a pidgin is not agreed upon by all researchers. For example, while the Heidelberger Forschungsprojekt Pidgindeutsch originally espoused the notion that Foreign Worker German is a "pidginized" form of German, its linguists nevertheless used the term "pidgin" with a number of clearly expressed reservations:

> The term Pidgin-German is not used within the parameters of this work in the strict sense of the term "pidgin," which was developed for specific contact-situations in colonial countries. . . . In using the term "pidgin-German" we are led by two particular considerations.
> *Firstly*, the term does not describe a *homogeneous* language, in the same way that "the German language does." Rather, it combines certain varieties of German that have specific linguistic and social dimensions in common and can be preliminarily set apart from other linguistic forms by the term "Pidgin-German."
> *Secondly*, the term refers to that variety of German which immigrant workers learn under similar social conditions. Thus, we have different learning contexts, in which a second language is learned under very different *individual* conditions from those contexts in which the great majority of a group of second-language learners learn a foreign language under the same or similar *social* conditions. In line with this difference we do not investigate the syntactic properties of the varieties of individuals, but rather of groups. We understand "Pidgin-Deutsch" as the more or less strongly

simplified German of foreign workers, who as a rule acquire it merely because of the exigencies of every day life in Germany through socially restricted contact with Germans and foreigners of other nationalities. The term applies essentially to the rudimentary German of foreign workers who must, on account of the need for understanding in order to cooperate in the workplace, use a variety of German, but who speak little or no German in their spare time, unless it is to solve the problems of daily needs, such as, shopping or a trip to the doctor's, etc. This, usually minimal, knowledge of German required to carry out a job is learned in routine interaction in the workplace. These usually superficial contacts, which are dictated by the job, usually lead to a socially functional use of a simplified variety of German, which is "frozen" at a particular level of linguistic competence.[14]

(Heidelberger Forschungsprojekt Pidgindeutsch 1975:81–83)

In other words, even through the project used the term "Pidgindeutsch," it did so in a specific sense.

Likewise, other researchers resist the use of the term "pidgin" to describe Foreign Worker German. For all the simplification strategies that Meisel (1975a) points to in Foreign Worker German, he does not classify it as a pidgin at all, but rather regards it as similar to foreigner talk. Foreigner talk is a simplified form of language (similar to caretaker speech or "motherese") used by native speakers of a language in conversation with foreigners, either as a marker of degradation, distance, and monopolization of the standard, according to Meisel (1975a) and Bodemann and Ostow (1975), or as a more positive marker of accommodation, according to Giles and Smith (1979) and Roche (1989).[15] Hinnenkamp (1984) also regards Foreign Worker German, not as a pidgin, but rather as the approximation by foreign workers of this simplified (and defective) foreigner-talk model they hear from native Germans. Similarly, Ferguson calls directly on the *process* of pidginization in explaining Foreign Worker German's development, yet nevertheless regards the German spoken to immigrant workers as foreigner talk and that spoken by them merely as "broken language": "The varieties of German used by and to immigrant workers are examples of foreigner talk and broken language phenomena, and the verbal interaction between native speakers and foreign workers are examples of the pidginization process at work" (1977:39). Nor, finally, do Bodemann and Ostow (1975) classify Foreign Worker German as a pidgin, regarding it as a "lingua franca," though they use the term "pseudo-pidgin" as well as their own, more colorful term, formed around the name of an exponent of the code, "Pfefferlesdeutsch") for the type of German that native speakers use toward foreign workers with restricted communicative abilities, that is, for foreigner talk or caretaker speech.

Blackshire-Belay provides us with another variant classification, since she also does not regard Foreign Worker German as a pidgin in the received sense of the term:

> The evidence from this study thus strongly suggests that the language of the foreign workers cannot be considered a pidgin at all but rather a "secondary hybrid" as referred to by Whinnom. It shows some features of a pidgin, such as zero subject, zero copula, the usage of an infinitive-like verb form, etc., but some of the pertinent factors that are expected in a pidgin and/or pidgin setting are lacking in this contact situation. For example, besides the infinitive-like verb form, a series of other verb forms and verb combinations is used. There is more inflectional morphology in the usage of these speakers than would normally be expected in a "true" pidgin. In reference to the social setting, the foreign worker community has not been totally cut off from the superstrate population, and thus exposure to the target language still prevails. Therefore in order for a pidgin to develop among these speakers, exposure to the superstrate language must be discontinued, and the contact among the adult foreign workers of different nationalities must remain constant.
>
> (1991:206)

On the other hand, Pavlou and Gilbert (1991) have no reservations about calling Foreign Worker German a pidgin, albeit of a particular kind. They classify it as an "industrial labor pidgin" and compare it with Foreign Worker Dutch and Foreign Worker French. They argue that Foreign Worker German is related to other traditional pidgins, specifically "slave pidgins" (for example, Guinea Coast and New World African Pidgin English, the precursor of the "Atlantic Creoles") and "indentured labor plantation and mining pidgins" (for example, Hawaiian Pidgin English, Town Bemba in Zambia, and Fangalo in South Africa). They submit that these three types of pidgin are "distinguished by the nature of the power relationship between overseers and laborers. The master-slave condition involves the smallest degree of voluntarism and the most coercion of those with the least power. Industrial laborers enter into the work relationship for almost exclusively economic reasons, which entails a much greater degree of voluntarism. Indenture or contractual labor lies somewhere in between" (1–2). They do, however, maintain a distinction between these types of pidgin and "full" or "extended" pidgins (for example, Tok Pisin in Papua New Guinea; Weskos, or Cameroon Pidgin English; and Chinook Jargon in the North American Pacific Northwest), though only on the basis of the latter's longevity and functional expansion. They argue that there is "no reason to separate industrial pidgins *qualitatively* from other pidgins," maintaining that "the factors in their genesis and development are different in degree, not in kind" (3). They provide the following list of factors that make Foreign Worker German "a textbook example of an industrial pidgin":

1. [I]t maintains good mutual intelligibility—in context—with non-pidginized varieties of German;
2. despite the variety of substrate languages involved, certain regularities of simplification appear everywhere the pidgin is spoken—the simplification is a function of linguistic universals and communicative needs;
3. interlocutor networks are highly restricted for many Gastarbeiter;
4. the ratio of native speakers to Gastarbeiter nevertheless remains high;
5. there are no indications that the basic economic conditions that have produced the pidgin will disappear.

(6–7)

Contrary to what Meisel (1975a) claims, Pavlou and Gilbert insist that Foreign Worker German's high degree of mutual intelligibility with the lexifier language (German) does not disqualify it as a pidgin, since a high degree of mutual intelligibility is a characteristic of pidgins generally. They also question the view that there is too much, and too frequent, contact between foreign workers and Germans for a pidgin in the usual sense to develop:

> The large absolute numbers of these people and the fact th[at] they are concentrated in urban centers makes it possible for many of them to survive in Germany by actually living in their own culture which has been transplanted into the host country. Many neighborhoods in German cities are reminiscent of the corresponding homelands of the people who live there. This situation enables a sizable number of them to function minimally in German society with very little or no knowledge of German as it is spoken by native speakers. Unemployed spouses, especially, may live for many years in Germany, totally isolated from the Germans and the German language. Since they perceive little pressure from the

society to acquire communicative skills in German, they do so only to the extent necessary. For them, the pidgin suffices for interethnic communication. Germans and non-Germans alike understand them, at least in context, so that they have very little incentive to "depidginize" their language.

(1991:5)

However, in my opinion, some of Pavlou and Gilbert's claims about the social environment are too strong. While segregation and ghettoization may have existed at appreciable levels into the 1980s, matters do seem to be improving on this level (see Chapter 2), so that true pidginization seems only a remote possibility; the linguistic behavior of second- and third-generation children gives no indication of either a pidgin stabilizing or of a creole developing, but rather indicates the acquisition of Standard (regional) German varieties. In fact, much of the argument about whether or not Foreign Worker German is a "true" pidgin comes down to the issue of whether immigrants have sufficient contact with mainstream Germans and access to native target forms.[16]

Blackshire-Belay suggests that there are "numerous occasions" on which foreigners are forced to communicate amongst themselves (with Foreign Worker German):

1. They constantly converse and exchange ideas in the residences (in the major cities there are still many of these in existence).
2. Foreigners of different nationalities are often invited to private gatherings at the home.
3. The foreigners meet at cook-outs and swim baths on the weekends.
4. Various centers bring the foreigners of different nationalities together by sponsoring activities for them, etc.

(1991:193)

Given this, if distance from Standard German is maintained, then Foreign Worker German could theoretically function as a pidgin, being used by immigrants in contact with one another who have no other language in common. In my own experience, Foreign Worker German varies from individual to individual and from group to group. The picture is not uniform because there is no homogeneous community of immigrants. While there are a few ethnic enclaves in certain large cities (such as Berlin or Munich), this picture is no longer consistent throughout Germany. As we saw in Chapter 2, since the late 1970s resident foreign workers no longer live isolated in barrack-style company residences, but have moved into better housing, not necessarily in any

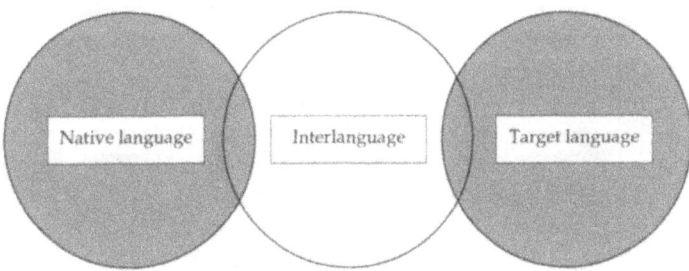

Figure 2. Interlanguage

particular quarter of a city. While this in itself does not guarantee social contact with Germans, it is certainly more promising than the isolation imposed by segregated company housing. At best, then, it seems problematic to characterize Foreign Worker German as a pidgin. The fact that pidgin characteristics of Foreign Worker German have been found in the research has implications for second- and subsequent-generation immigrants, and we shall have cause to discuss these later in this chapter.

Overlapping Systems: Pidgins, Creoles, Interlanguages, and Xenolects

Part of the classificational dilemma lies in the essential overlap between contact-language development and general second-language development. All of these dynamic and nonstandard varieties can be grouped together without controversy under the term "interim languages" (see Kutsch and Desgranges 1985), and, regarded as such, they have many features in common. We can illustrate the hypothetical relationship between any interlanguage[17] (IL) and the native language (NL) and target language (TL) to which it is related as in Figure 2. While there is overlap between the interlanguage and both the NL and the TL, the interlanguage also displays a significant proportion of rules that are independent of either of these. The essential question here is, what types of rules does the nonoverlapping area of interlanguage contain? In Meisel's (1977) terms, this area contains rules of restrictive ($\approx$ fossilizing) and elaborative ($\approx$ progressive) simplification; thus, the interlanguage has rules that are neither exactly like the NL nor like the TL in form, though, of course, some do agree with TL rules. With favorable conditions for L2 acquisition, the elaborative rules facilitate progression

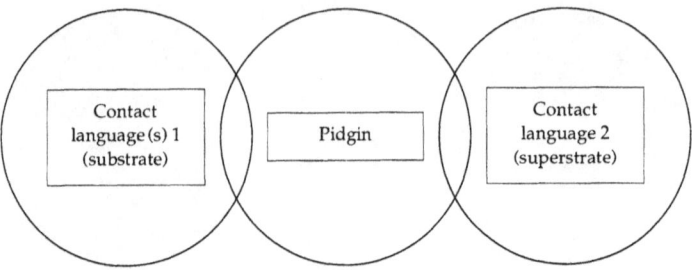

Figure 3. Pidgin

along the acquisitional stages toward the TL. In other words, all things being equal, simplification is not normally a permanent strategy in the language-acquisition process; rather, complexification is the norm. However, when this is not the case, and restrictive simplification is the norm, fossilization occurs. Meisel argues, in fact, that the difference between the two strategies is also a major difference between (native-generated) foreigner talk and L2 interlanguage: foreigner talk does not avail itself of elaborative simplification.

The parallels between pidginization and general second-language acquisition may become clearer if we conceptualize the development of a pidgin in a similar way (see Figure 3). In this situation, the new contact variety again features rules that resemble neither the first nor the second contact language. It is most likely that the bulk of rules in this dialect conform to Meisel's restrictive simplification strategies. Should the situation stabilize and spread from individual to individual, so that it becomes the norm for a particular group of people, then a stable pidgin could develop, which would expand both formally and functionally—though in a direction different from either the first or second contact language.

A creole (that is, a nativized pidgin) could hypothetically develop out of the pidgin if the contents of the non-overlapping area expand to meet the greater communicative demands of a new generation in need of a native language. Thus, the middle section would necessarily also contain rules of elaboration. However, these rules of elaboration do not progress in the direction of the superstrate language, but branch off in an independent direction. The system would still display overlap with the substrate and superstrate language, but the constellation of features within the non-overlapping segment would change. Thus Figure 3 could be adapted to account for the relationship of a creole to its superstrate and substrate languages (see Figure 4). Diagramma-

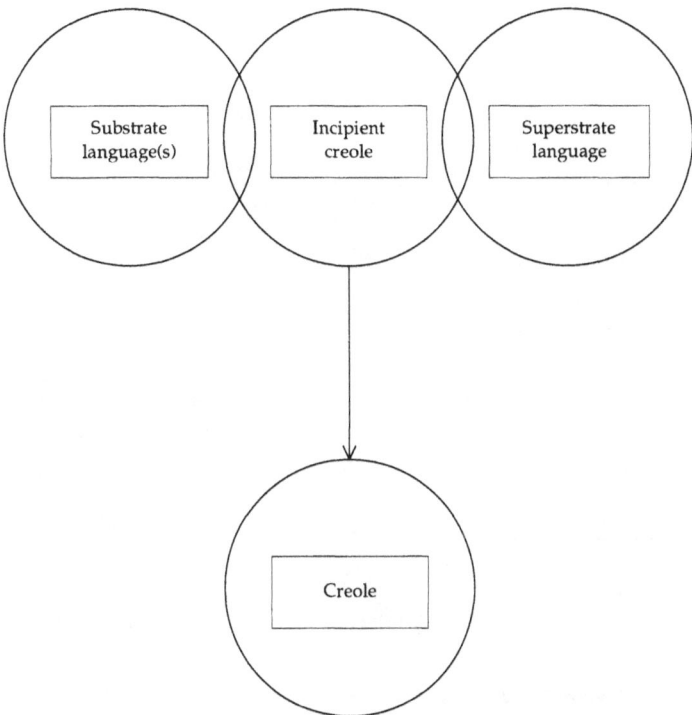

Figure 4. Creole

tically, as shown in Figure 5, Foreign Worker German displays a similar relationship to the NL and the German TL. In other words, while the system of Foreign Worker German overlaps both the NL and the German TL (usually the local, not the national standard, variety), it also displays rules that resemble neither of these languages, such as sentences with missing subjects or uninflected verbs, as discussed at the beginning of this chapter. The constellation of rules in the non-overlapping area of Figure 5 resembles interlanguages, pidgins, and creoles in that this constellation allows for both restrictive and elaborative simplification. However, what else it contains and the relative preponderance of strategies depends very much on the individual circumstances of the speaker, and it is clear that no overall direction of development can be predicted for all immigrants, but rather that the circumstances of particular groups and particular individuals must be taken into account. First-generation immigrants with highly restricted contacts are likely to rely heavily on strategies of restrictive simplifica-

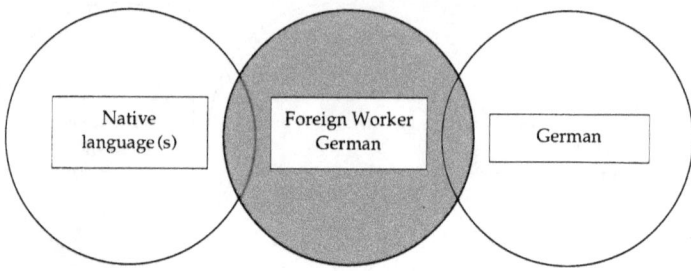

Figure 5. Foreign Worker German

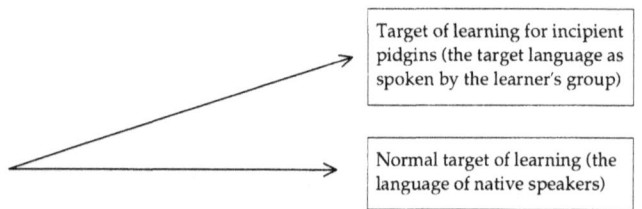

Figure 6. Normal Second-Language Development vs. Incipient Pidgin

tion; possibly, as time wears on, they will call less and less on strategies of elaborative simplification, causing fossilization and genuine pidginization (Blackshire-Belay's Type 1). First-generation immigrants with extensive social contacts with Germans are more likely to progress toward competence in the local target, calling upon strategies of elaborative simplification, though no doubt retaining a large amount of interference from the L1 (Blackshire-Belay's Type 2). Gilbert (1983:176) illustrates these two options as shown in Figure 6. Normal progression toward the target language is represented along the bottom line, while speakers who have the language of the immigrant group as a target veer off from the native target, developing an incipient pidgin. As we will see in the next section, such a development is at least theoretically possible for the second generation in Germany, though, in fact, prevailing social conditions make it a highly unlikely eventuality.

The Second Generation and Creolization

Whether we talk about pidgins or about interlanguages, second-generation immigrants have a different starting point from first-generation immigrants, and therefore display a radically different constellation of features in their language that are also highly dependent on their social

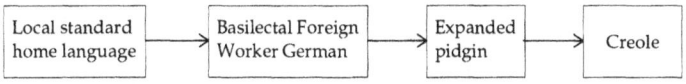

Figure 7. *Theoretical Progression to Creole*

situation. Many of them start with a quasi-bilingual background: their parents speak both the home language and Pidgindeutsch. Given the right amount of contact with native speakers of German, and provided there is no conflict at home about learning German (which is, in any case, usually to the detriment of the parents' home language), and given a certain degree of motivation that is predicated upon adequate educational and social opportunities, second-generation immigrants should and do acquire the local variety of German. This often features some direct or substratum effect, usually on the level of pronunciation, from the home language of their parents. Only in the total absence of these conditions, however, where there is absolutely no opportunity or motivation to acquire a native version of German, when children are kept at home by immigrant parents and not allowed to interact with Germans[18] or when there are absolutely no Germans in the area in which they live, is it at all possible that the children could end up with a more expanded version of their parents' pidgin. Such eventualities are highly unlikely, and even if there were the odd isolated case, whether or not this would then go on to creolize is dependent again upon the social factors we have discussed, in particular upon the degree of separation of the immigrant community from mainstream German speakers and from German society in general. Thus we might allow for the theoretical progression diagrammed in Figure 7, from the home language to a highly reduced or basilectal variety to an expanded pidgin and on to a creole. Considering the changes in the social position of foreign workers in Germany since the late 1970s, however, creolization has to be considered an unlikely outcome, since any group of foreign children going on to develop a creole as a native language in this way would have to live in a separate and fairly large community. Rather, the overwhelming majority of normal second- and third-generation children go on to complete acquisition of the target. Much more likely is an eventual kind of substratum effect, reminiscent of what developed in immigrant Jewish and Italian children in New York (see Labov 1972), where basic structures are acquired while innovating an ethnolectal variety, in which phonetic features ("accent") and lexical items alone provide the "ethnic overlay."

Educational Success of the Second Generation and the Notion of "Semilingualism"

While to my knowledge there are no figures available, one could conjecture that, provided they are exposed to good linguistic role models, the vast majority of second-generation speakers who are either born in Germany or move to Germany at a fairly young age (before puberty), do develop a competent variety of German as their first language.

However, a perpetual lament amongst certain educators has been that some immigrant children end up with neither their parents' home language nor an accepted form of German, a condition which Skutnabb-Kangas and Toukamaa (1976) have termed "semilingualism." Discussions of this type are always very dangerous, however, since they tend, either explicitly or indirectly, to equate inability to speak the standard dialect with cognitive deficiency, or at least to perpetuate the myth that "different = inferior."

In a study of the linguistic performance of Turkish-German, bilingual, school-aged students in Berlin, for example, Steinmüller provides an informative profile of "the typical," second-generation immigrant child, extracted from a questionnaire developed as part of the model experiment dealing with Turkish-German bilingual children:

> The student was born in Germany as a younger child of many children. He attended neither kindergarten nor any other type of preschool institution, but rather was cared for by older siblings, until he entered the *Grundschule*. Until entering the school of the model experiment, he spent his school year in a German standard classroom. He has German friends, with whom he gets together in his free time, however, he belongs to neither a German [n]or a nationally-mixed organization or club. German television programs are watched almost daily, Turkish film videos are watched several hours a week. Reading material consists for the most part of German comic books. The family, as a rule, spends its vacation in Germany. The child functions—particularly for the parents—frequently as a translator in contact with the German environment. The biography of this "model student" shows the significant characteristics which lead to subtractive bilingualism, that is, where the learner does not possess sufficiently developed and differentiated linguistic abilities in either of his two languages.
>
> (1991:11)

The last sentence of this passage is very troubling. Steinmüller found that the German and Turkish language abilities of the children in his study were widely heterogeneous and very often inadequate for the demands of secondary education and beyond. Yet, a significant finding of his study is that both Turkish and German children make the same kinds of errors in German, and that "there is not one element that causes difficulties exclusively for Turkish students" (3). Thus, to my way of understanding, his findings once again support the observation that the influence of the first language on the second is not the major cause of errors and deviant linguistic behavior. What Steinmüller's study really shows is that the German acquired by the immigrant children in his study is not the middle-class, educated, standard form preferred in schools. This finding could equally apply to many non-middle-class mainstream German children. The problem of Steinmüller's study is that it fails to point this out explicitly and, thus, makes his findings available as fuel for the "difference = deficit" interpretation, painfully reminiscent of the controversy following Bereiter and Engelmann's (1966) ultimately damaging application of Bernstein's theories of the 1950s and 1960s to African American children in the United States—even though Bernstein's ideas had been so ably (and, one would have hoped, conclusively) shot down by the earlier work of Labov (e.g., 1970) and discussed directly in Germany by Dittmar (1973).

Steinmüller (1991) uses his study to argue for the importance of a solid home-language base in the development of proficiency in the L2. While he specifically mentions the adequacy of the cognitive abilities of his subjects on the one hand—"The children possess the cognitive abilities commensurate with their age groups"—at the same time and in the same sentence, he makes a direct link between inability to speak (prestige, standard) German and inadequacy of cognitive processes: "however, they lack the means in two languages to process mentally and communicate that which they would be capable of doing using linguistic signs" (11). One is left with the dangerous impression that speaking nonstandard German is indicative of some sort of mental deficiency.

An important finding of Steinmüller's study is that "the acquisition of the second language of German is most successful for students who have a secure foundation in the development of the first language" (12). Consequently, Steinmüller proposes that they should be encouraged to develop first in their home language and that more attention should be paid in school to their acquisition of German as a second language. These findings accord well with the opinions of Skutnabb-Kangas (1986), who has long advocated both the promotion of the home language and preschool education in the second language as a means to promote development in bilingual children. In support of such measures, Skutnabb-Kangas (1990:19) reports a study in Sweden that shows that Finnish children whose basic, nine-year schooling was conducted in Finnish know Finnish almost as well as Finns educated in Finland and that their overall level of achievement is comparable to that of Swedes. Corson (1993:84–85) shows that children who were given their early schooling in their L1 were going on to attend university in significantly higher numbers than those who were not being instructed in their L1. It would appear that there is definitely a positive correlation between home-language instruction and *educational* success, but this is a long way from suggesting that a lack of standard language ability is equivalent to *cognitive* deficiency. One cannot help but feel that the term "semilingualism" is a most unfortunate one. Much more work needs to be done on the social factors influencing language acquisition and educational success.

In a study of the acquisition of German as a second language by Turkish schoolchildren, Jürgen Biehle (1987) places great emphasis on the role of social factors. He demonstrates the importance of the type of language instruction received, of the role of the teacher, and of specific cooperation between the school and the parental home. With the second generation as with the first, as Biehle emphasizes, contact with German friends is important in successful language acquisition, which is consonant also with the role of peers in language development (see Labov 1972). Another important factor for Biehle is the parental attitude toward school and learning. Moreover, he was able to confirm the findings of Keim (1978, 1984) that a critical stance toward political and religious relations in Turkey and the feeling of acceptance in the German society (by having German friends and contacts) lead to more successful language acquisition. In sum, the importance of social factors, in particular the family situation, is not to be underestimated in the language acquisition of the second generation.[19]

Once again, we must emphasize that it is still an open question whether subsequent generations of immigrants will be isolated enough from the mainstream and will interact with each other enough to develop an expanded pidgin or, indeed, a creole. At the moment, the possibility for creolization seems remote, because of improvements in school systems, teaching methods, and social conditions. All of the indications are that immigrant children do develop a fluent form of German, albeit not necessarily the prestige, standard language. This is consistent with developments in the United States, where a high level of assimilation has usually taken place by the third generation (see Conklin and Lourie 1983). That immigrant children fail in school is most certainly not due solely (or even primarily) to linguistic factors, but rather to other social conditions prevailing in society.

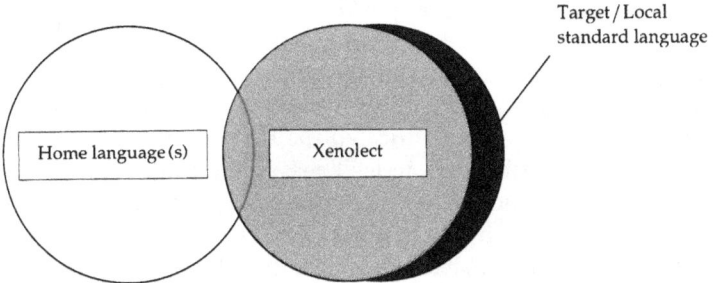

Figure 8. Xenolect

Xenolect

A final possibility for the development of Foreign Worker German must be considered, this time with a view to the future and with particular emphasis on the function of language as an identity marker. We have argued that the pidgin-creole hypothesis seems to have become a less and less likely scenario for Foreign Worker German in the past decade; however, this does not mean that it will necessarily die out altogether. There is a further potential outcome of contact between immigrant languages and a standard language variety that may well apply to the second and subsequent generations of foreign workers speaking German. This is the possibility that a "xenolect" might emerge. Holm defines xenolects as "slightly foreignized varieties spoken natively" (1988:10). Hence, a xenolect, see Figure 8, can be conceptualized differently from the interlanguage varieties diagrammed earlier. This is partly because we might regard a xenolect as the product of contact that has already led to the acquisition of a native variety. In this instance the area where there is no overlap with the local standard variety is very small, as is the area where there is overlap with the home language(s). The majority of the dialect is in fact consonant with the native variety, or, in other words, there is no significant linguistic restructuring.[20]

Such a xenolect would superficially resemble a creole (and, thus, would come under the heading of a "creoloid" variety) in that it may be, for example, morphologically somewhat simpler than the native variety; however, it cannot be a true creole since it has not undergone the significant restructuring required.[21] It would of course, linguistically speaking, be comparable to any other nonstandard (regional or social) dialect, although the source of those features that make it different from the standard would be the direct or indirect external influence of the home languages of the speakers' immigrant community, rather than, for example, differences in pronunciation caused by a language-internal phonetic shift. In general, it is important to point out that if we took regional colloquial dialects as a point of comparison (rather than the standard, middle-class, educated dialect) many of the differences would be less noticeable and, indeed, less foreign looking.

Although to my knowledge there are no documented examples of German xenolects (such as a distinctive Kreuzberg immigrant dialect in Berlin),[22] there are precedents for the development of xenolects in other West European, industrial immigrant communities. For example, there have been published reports in Sweden of an incipient variety of Swedish, *Rinkebysvenska*, developing in Rinkeby, a suburb of Stockholm with a large majority of non-Swedish, ethnically and linguistically diverse children. It is useful to discuss Rinkebysvenska in detail, given the potential for such developments in Germany.

Immigrant children's Swedish has been variously described as not differing significantly from that of their Swedish peers; as "poor" and deficient, resulting from incomplete learning, and inadequate to express elementary linguistic needs; and as fulfilling the immigrant children's linguistic needs, yet "odd," "different," and "difficult to understand."[23] Kotsinas suggests that it is not impossible for the Swedish of one and the same individual to be characterized in all three ways, depending on the contexts in which it is used. For example, it might be considered as perfectly acceptable Swedish in informal contexts, poor and insufficient in school, and adequate but deviant when used with other immigrant children in normal interaction (Kotsinas 1988:131).

Kotsinas maintains that in Sweden today conditions are theoretically ripe for the development of a creole, since "broken" Swedish is used as a means of communication between adults and children of diverse immigrant backgrounds and of different mother tongues. Indeed, she suggests that "[f]or many children, school is the only place where they hear Swedish spoken by natives" (1988:133) and that in these communities the native speakers may in fact be in a very small minority. Moreover, teachers who teach immigrant children tend often to speak a mixture of foreigner talk and teacher talk, and might not themselves, therefore, serve as adequate models of Standard Swedish (133). In a similar fashion to researchers in Germany, Kotsinas (1981, 1982, 1984a, 1984b, 1991) has shown that the interlanguage used by six adult immigrant speakers of Swedish (five Greeks and one Pole) displayed both general features of learner varieties and similar linguistic characteristics to pidgins of various varieties, including limited vocabulary, omission of certain function words, reduction of the inventory of prepositions, almost total absence of inflections, few or no subordinate clauses, deviant word order, and considerable variation across speakers (1988: 133). Lexical shortages are accommodated by, for example, semantic over-extensions, repetitions, circumlocutions, and paraphrases, while grammatical features are accommodated by, for example, analytical (lexical) expressions in place of synthetic (morphological) ones (134).

Presumably using her study of adult language as the putative source of input for the second and subsequent generations, Kotsinas argues that it might be theoretically possible for second-generation immigrants to develop a creole version of Swedish based on the pidgin-like adult varieties (135). However, she points out that "the emergence of a creole presupposes a distance, socially, psychologically and/or geographically, to speakers of the base language" (135). While such barriers do exist to a certain extent between native Swedes and immigrants, school education, migration within Sweden to areas with fewer immigrants, radio, and television constitute just some of the factors that mitigate this separation. However, she continues, it is not likely that all second-generation immigrants will develop a nativelike variety. Rather, she expects they would develop "a variety with lexical, that is, analytic,[24] expressions where Swedish children prefer morphological means, simplifications within the opaque,[25] that is, difficult, parts of the grammar, a certain number of repetitions and paraphrases, and perhaps also, as in creoles, additions to the vocabulary; for example, by loans and translations of lexical items from the languages spoken in the area, all used without hesitation, just like an 'ordinary' language. Such a variety might also be very fluent" (135).

The social role of Rinkeby Swedish is much more revealing than its scant formal details. In Rinkeby, children are well aware that they speak a variety of Swedish that is much different from native varieties—to such an extent that they have developed names for it, such as *Rinkebyska* ("Rinkebyish") and *Rinkebysvenska* ("Rinkeby Swedish") (135–36). In comparison with standard, middle-class, educated Swedish, this variety is linguistically simplified in terms of grammar, though it contains some elaborating features, which are mostly lexical. The speakers themselves characterize it as "different," "more tougher" [sic], "filled with slang," "secret," and not used in the presence of adults (136). It is on the level of pronunciation, however, that Kotsinas detects the most striking differences from native varieties. Vowel quantity and vowel quality both differ from Standard Swedish and the distinction between long and short syllable seems to be "diminished or erased," while certain phonemes are pronounced more distinctly than normal; prosody contains both native and nonnative features (136). Moreover, as she points out, this pronunciation does not seem to characterize one ethnic group: "Remarkably, it is almost impossible for a native Swede to guess the speaker's mother tongue, that is, the accents seem to have converged into one, signaling 'Swede with an immigrant background'" (136). Vocabulary is also a mixture of both Swedish and generally foreign elements; for example, *chavles*, which is Romani for "thief," is found as well as *ayde len*, which is a mixture of Greek and Turkish and means "get lost." Furthermore, certain Swedish words and idioms are shifted semantically; in particular, the Swedish words for *go* and *come* are semantically extended (136). The grammar deviates quite frequently from Standard (written and spoken) Swedish, especially with typologically marked features such as gender, agreement, word order, and the use of prepositions. To illustrate the stability of the variety, Kotsinas points out that "[c]ertain deviations seem so fixed that even some Swedish children and, occasionally, even teachers and youth center staff use them. So, for example, a boy, corrected by his teacher in a matter of grammar, once answered: 'What you say is not correct in Rinkebyish'" (136).

Thus an important function of Rinkebysvenska is to mark group membership. Kotsinas suggests that it "might . . . serve as an ethnic group variety similar to Black English in the United States . . . : [it] is used by young people only, and in more pregnant form by some individuals, mostly immigrant boys, than others. Quite in accordance with the speakers' own statements, it seems to be used more frequently in certain contexts, for example at the youth center, than in others, for example in classrooms" (131–36).

In Sweden, as in many parts of Germany, it is unlikely that a sufficiently large proportion of immigrant children will be kept separate from the mainstream long enough to promote the development of a truly restructured creole, but Rinkebysvenska clearly bears an important function as a social semiotic. For this reason, and given its relatively slight differences from mainstream Swedish, I would prefer to classify Rinkebysvenska as a *xenolect*, which relies not on radical restructuring, but on a small but symbolically significant amount of influence from immigrant language(s) to render it identifiably different from the standard. To this extent Rinkebysvenska has much in common with German youth speech, or *Jugendsprache*, which is a well-known and well-researched phenomenon whose major function is as a signifier of group identity (see Henne 1986; Schlobinski, Kohl, and Luding 1993; and the ongoing discussion in *Schatzkammer*, the American journal for teachers of German).

As we have said above, given the encouraging signs of progress in the German immigrant community in terms of social integration and education, it seems most unlikely that Foreign Worker German will develop into a true creole. Its function as a social marker of distinction from mainstream Germans, however, is another matter entirely. We have seen time and again in working-class communities that stigmatized forms of speech are maintained in the face of overall change toward the standard, precisely because they serve as solidarity markers and markers of group identity (see Milroy 1987 and discussions in Labov 1994). To my knowledge, no work has been done on immigrant youth varieties of German,[26] and, of course, it is too early to tell what the linguistic developments will be in the third generation of immigrant workers in Germany. This is clearly a promising avenue for future research.

The Creole Continuum

Rather than adopting an "all-or-nothing" approach to the data and trying to make them fit neatly under one heading—pidgin, creole, learner dialect, or xenolect—I have argued that we need to recognize that it is normal in any language situation for multiple varieties to be used at the same time. Ferguson (1959) pointed this out long ago in his discussion of the symbolic use of H(igh) and L(ow) varieties of language in all diglossic communities, both within one language and in bilingual or multilingual communities. In other words, while we concentrate on the range of language used in contact situations here, such continua are in fact part of all language use, and not merely limited to language-contact situations.

The importance of the fact that language varieties naturally coexist in a continuum is illustrated very well by Mufwene (1994), writing about Gullah, a contact language spoken on the coastal islands of Georgia and South Carolina. In considering the processes of decreolization and language death with reference to Gullah, Mufwene questions the received notion of the rectilinear development of creoles from basic (basilectal) forms through intermediate (mesolectal) forms to standardlike (acrolectal)[27] forms that end up merging with the superstrate or lexifier language. Figure 9 diagrams this hypothetical relationship, where there is a supposed rectilinear development that entails the loss of the basilectal, or reduced forms, as acrolectal ones develop. Mufwene's main objection to this assumed development is the fact that basilectal, mesolectal, and acrolectal varieties *coexist* in the Gullah population and that, contrary to expectations, there is no evidence of change (or attrition of features) in Gullah in the past fifty years. The basic point to be made

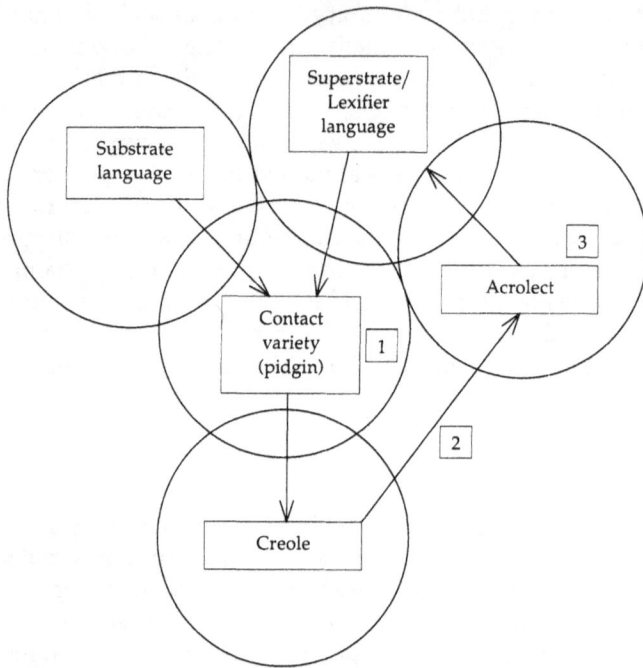

Figure 9. Typical Development of Creoles

here is that "continua similar to the creole continuum exist in other language or speech communities, especially where there is diglossia, as in France, the United Kingdom, and the United States" (71). There is no general progression toward the acrolect that necessarily entails the loss of more basic lects.

In Germany, all possible varieties of Foreign Worker German—basilectal, mesolectal, and acrolectal—also coexist, and this, too, is a natural language situation. At one extreme, foreign workers speak acrolectal varieties that are close to the (local) standard and are the product of successful second language acquisition. At the other end of the scale, pidginlike basilectal varieties exist and persist because of linguistic and social separation. In the middle are a host of mesolectal varieties. It is neither inevitable that speakers progress toward the standard, nor is it inevitable that their language fossilizes at a certain stage of development; this all depends on the particular constellation of factors conditioning the individual.

It is the strength of social boundaries that will dictate to what extent these varieties are kept separate and different. As the Rinkeby study shows, this is by no means a unidirectional, top-down process. Whereas access can be denied from above by the prestige sectors of society, communities have also been shown to preserve stigmatized and ridiculed varieties because of their function as markers of identity and group solidarity. There are many examples of this in the literature. Mufwene points out that this has been the case with Gullah, which has made slight accommodations and adjustments to the mainstream dialect, but which has not undergone radical restructuring (81). The same persistence of stigmatized dialect forms as markers of identity has been observed on Martha's Vineyard (Labov 1972) and the Outer Banks of North Carolina (Wolfram and Schilling-Estes 1994, 1995). Since the maintenance of such forms depends on such issues as vitality, identity, loyalty, and whether social networks open up across racial and ethnic lines (Mufwene 1994:86), it would not be surprising if stigmatized Foreign Worker German forms were to persist across time (and perhaps particularly with immigrant youth). It is clearly too early to tell at this point. Moreover, while sociolinguists have looked closely at the "grass roots" aspects of language loyalty and identity, there is also no doubt that with immigrant communities the intellectual elite often has a decisive role to play in the promotion or demotion of language varieties, as will be discussed in the following chapter.

The Language of Later Generations

From my current theoretical and geographical vantage point, it seems unlikely that Foreign Worker German will persist in any highly restructured form beyond the second generation. If we accept that Germany actually is an Einwanderungsland, despite the many protestations cataloged in Chapter 1, then the linguistic abilities of foreign-worker children will no doubt develop in a similar fashion to those of second-, third-, and subsequent-generation immigrants in other immigration countries, such as Australia and the United States. In the United States, as Conklin and Lourie (1983:159-83) point out, while first-generation immigrants rarely become fluent bilinguals, the second generation, their children, tend to be typically diglossic, speaking their parents' mother tongue in the home, the neighborhood, and religious contexts and speaking English with native or near-native ability in education or at work; by contrast, the third generation is often monolingual in English, having English as their true native language. While there are no figures available at present, especially with reference to bilingual ability, the progression of third-generation immigrants to higher educational levels in Germany (see Chapter 2) would seem to suggest that they, too, are developing native competence in German.

In order for a nationwide ethnic variety of German to exist (let alone a pidgin or a creole), immigrants would have to suffer, for example, the same kind of large-scale segregation and social discrimination that the African slaves did in Jamaica, and this is clearly not the case. Most foreign workers' children in the Federal Republic have access to native-speaker models, and the majority of school systems are developing or have developed integrative programs of educational provision for foreign workers' children. Even in parts of Bavaria, where segregated classes persist, it is unlikely that generations of immigrant children will be completely segregated and deprived of native models of language. Thus, while pidginization and creolization remain a *theoretical* possibility, this development seems highly unlikely on a practical level. Because of local constraints on interaction with native speakers, pockets of basilectal varieties may persist within families (cf. the second and third generation of Pakistani women in Britain) or even in certain concentrated neighborhoods, but this would hardly persist on a broad enough level to promote a recognized creole variety.

Where Foreign Worker German might well persist, however, is in the literary medium, as a form of identity marking. We shall have much to say about the changing attitudes of immigrant writers to Gastarbeiterdeutsch in the next chapter. Suffice it to say here, however, that this symbolic use is again hardly likely to be on a scale large enough to effect any real restructuring of an immigrant variety.

Recent Changes in *Gastarbeiterlinguistik*

While we have concentrated up to this point on the issue of the varietal status of Foreign Worker German, which is of central importance to the present work, for completeness' sake we need to acknowledge that Gastarbeiterlinguistik has changed its focus in the past decade, and that structural and linguistic emphases have given way to interpretive and intercultural considerations. Hinnenkamp has divided Gastarbeiterlinguistik into three major phases:

Phase 1: Gastarbeiterdeutsch as a code to be discovered: What is different, what is lacking with reference to the target language? (Clyne 1968, Orlovic-Schwarzwald 1978)

Phase 2: Gastarbeiterdeutsch as a sociolinguistic phenomenon: What extralinguistic factors condition undirected language acquisition? (Heidelberger Forschungsprojekt Pidgindeutsch 1975)

Phase 3: Gastarbeiterdeutsch as an interactional problem and product: How do communication processes between native and nonnative speakers condition the acquisition and communication process? (for example, Kutsch and Desgranges 1985)

(1990:284)

In line with the general linguistic trends of the seventies and early eighties, approaches to the description of learner dialect neglected the *meaning* of learner utterances in favor of their *form*. In the seventies, analyses of learner-dialect utterances tended to concentrate on describing surface syntactic structures and on comparing them with the standard form of the native and the target languages, probably under the influence of standard contrastive analysis methodology with its focus on theory, rather than on practice, such as that outlined by James (1980). However, from the mid-eighties onward, a growing interest in the analysis of communication strategy led people to the realization that, since formal descriptions were merely product-oriented, attempting to reconstruct the original "communication strategy" of the speaker from the point of view of the source language would lead to a radically different outcome, which would necessarily concentrate on the process involved in the development of the utterance (see Dittmar 1984: 243). Such analyses are in line with findings in alternative types of contrastive analysis and language-transfer studies that recognize that what is transferred by learners in the production of a target-language utterance is not always a simple structural feature (e.g., in French adjectives usually follow nouns, therefore French speakers put adjectives after nouns in English) but rather that we need to consider the role of semantic, pragmatic, and sociolinguistic aspects in the development of communicative competence in another language. Thus, understanding how learners communicate is not merely a question of counting gaps or additions, nor just a matter of describing how learners learn to form sentences, but, more importantly, it is a matter of how they learn to *mean*.

This shift in emphasis led to some dramatic changes in approach by some of the leading researchers in the field. For example, Dittmar, Klein, Rieck, and others, known for the Heidelberger Forschungsprojekt Pidgindeutsch, switched their focus away from the description of syntactic regularities in Foreign Worker German, with Standard German as the reference point, toward classifying the learner varieties as "expressively deficient" or "expressively equivalent" to the target language. This change in approach constitutes for Hinnenkamp (1990: 283) a great step forward over earlier, largely form-driven studies, since it represents *inter*action with immigrant learners of German and attention to interactional functionality and dysfunctionality in the context of communication *between* immigrants and native speakers of German. Dittmar sums up the basic objectives of such research thus:

1. How does a learner organize meanings at a particular learning stage?
2. What semantic function do various forms assume in a particular system?
3. As more and more target language features are gradually acquired, how are learner meanings adapted and reorganized to fulfill new functions?

(1984:246)

Finding the answers to such questions involves the application of all the tools of pragmatic analysis as well as those of semantics and syntax. Typically, researchers call upon a functional grammatical theory, such as componential analysis or theme-rheme/topic-comment analysis, Gricean principles of cooperation, and the like (246). Recent studies dealing with undirected language acquisition in Europe have emphasized the analysis of such semantic concepts as modality (Dittmar et al. 1988), temporality (Stutterheim 1986, Kuhberg 1986, Dittmar and Kuhberg 1988), and spatial reference (Dittmar and Reich 1987). Work has also been carried out on the communicative strategies of migrants in interethnic interaction (Dittmar and Stutterheim 1985).

Intended Meaning and Prepositional Usage

As just mentioned, the investigation of transfer from the learner's L1 has also changed its focus. In order to illustrate this change of approach to Foreign Worker German, which now takes into account more than surface interlingual transfer, I should like to discuss here an analysis of a number of prepositional constructions produced in the context of verbs of motion by Polish immigrant workers speaking German (Fennell 1991). My focus here is not primarily on the structural differences between Polish and German, but rather on the semantic reconstruction of the speakers' intended utterances in the study. It will be shown that, on a purely surface, formal level, there is no direct relation between the actual form produced and the German target language and that, at most, there is a tenuous relation between these produced forms and the L1. However, if we reconstruct what the speaker intended to mean, using the L1 as our starting point, the L1-IL-L2 relationship becomes much clearer, and we gain insight into the strategy used in producing the actual utterances.

The four subjects in this part of the study are radically different from each other and display a wide range of linguistic ability with regard to the use of verbs of motion in German. Sascha is the least able to communicate in German: in all of the recordings, spanning two years, he never uses a single verb of motion with a preposition. Antek represents another basic stage: he has little German to begin with, but takes an intensive course at the Goethe Institute during the project, so that he also contrasts with the others in no longer being a pure product of natural, undirected language learning. We will focus specifically on his utterances, for reasons given below. Janka represents a fascinating in-between stage: she uses almost no prepositions with verbs of motion during the first year of recording, her primary strategy being instead to indicate spatial relations by juxtaposing a thematic noun phrase with a relatum, usually another noun phrase following the verb:

also diese man kommt diese wand
"well this man comes this wall"
(≈ "Well, the man comes up to the wall.")

Eventually, Janka starts introducing prepositions, beginning with *zu*, then *von*:

*diese hund eh gehen eh **zum** diese zimmer*
"this dog eh go eh to the this room"
(≈ "The dog goes into the room.")

*diese hund schnell eh **von** trappe gehen eh **zu** die eh **zu** der mann*
"this dog quickly eh from steps goes eh to the eh to the man"
(≈ "The dog quickly goes down the steps and up to the man.")

Finally, Ela, who is in closer contact with Germans and who has reading knowledge of German at the beginning of the recordings, displays a rich array of prepositions and shows every sign of progressing rapidly in the direction of the target language, though she still uses nonstandard morphology. These four speakers can be seen to illustrate the type of continuum we discussed above, from basilectal through mesolectal toward acrolectal forms of German.

Antek is the most interesting informant from our point of view, since at first his preposition usage deviated in a seemingly chaotic way from Standard (written) German, until we probe deeper into what he intended to say by making reference to the context and to his native language. What I wish to demonstrate here is that there is no straightforward one-to-one relationship between his native language and his actual utterances, nor is there a gradual progression from the native language via this interlanguage to the target language. Instead, it would appear that there are conceptual overlaps influencing Antek's lexical choices, and, if we read between the lines of his native language and his frequent self-corrections to find the right preposition, we discover that what at first seems like chaos is behavior based on conceptual choices.

For the sake of brevity, we will focus our analysis on the seemingly haphazard use of *mit* ("with") in the following two original utterances by Antek:

(1) *kann ich mit diese bäume gehen auf die erste und . . . springen hier*
"can I with these trees go on the first and . . . jump here"
(≈ "I can go from this tree to the first one and jump here.")

(2) *er hat mit dem fenster . . . mitgekommen dieses raum*
"he has with the window withcome this room"
(≈ "He came through the window into the room.")

In Standard (native) German these sentences may be rendered as follows:

(1a) *kann ich von diesem Baum gehen auf den ersten . . . und hier springen*
"can I from this tree go to the first one . . . and here jump"

(2a) *er ist durch das Fenster . . . hereingekommen in diesen Raum*
"he is through the window come in into this room"

In the case of sentence (1) (*mit diese bäume*), the seeming incongruence between *mit*, which has the basic meaning "with," and the intended *von* ("from") is explained as a semantic expansion based on the Polish preposition *z*, which can have both the meanings "with" or "from" (out of/off of)." These two meanings are differentiated in Polish by using the preposition with nouns in different cases for each: in the instrumental for the former and in the genitive for the latter. Since German does not have an instrumental case (or, for that matter, a true genitive, at least in the spoken language), these meanings coalesce for the L2 learner in German, leading to the generalization that *mit* = Polish z, expressing both the concept "with" and "motion from off of," as shown in Figure 10.

With sentence (2) (*mit dem fenster mitgekommen*), a similar strategy can be observed. The concept "motion through" can be expressed in Polish by using the preposition *przez* with a noun in the accusative case or, in certain circumstances, just by using a noun in the instrumen-

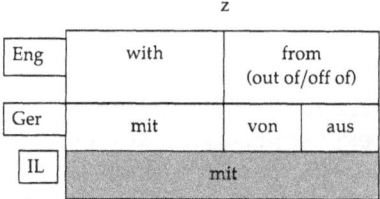

Figure 10. Polish z *vs. German* mit

tal case alone. In literary Polish "motion through" can be expressed by *przez* + accusative (*przez okno*, "through the window"); however, "motion through," e.g., "a wood" or "fields," can also be expressed by the instrumental alone (*oknem*, "through the window"; *lasem*, "through the woods"; *polami*, "through the fields").[29] In this instance, it appears that the L1 concept "through" has been extended, leading to an underlying instrumental form akin to *oknem*. Since the instrumental overlaps partially with the meaning "with" in Polish, this then licenses the use of *mit* for "through" in the subject's interlanguage. Thus **mit** *dem fenster* conveys the intended meaning of *oknem* (***durch** das Fenster*), thereby extending the concept of *mit*.

Thus the Polish speaker has not simply transferred a Polish preposition or, indeed, morphological ending into German, but rather he has transferred part of the meaning of the Polish instrumental onto the German preposition *mit*, thus extending its meaning, which is a universal strategy in interethnic communication.[30]

The point of this brief illustration is that, rather than focusing on the purely contrastive analytical, surface structural contrasts between German and Polish, later studies of Foreign Worker German concentrate on strategies of communication (such as extension of meaning, overgeneralization, etc.) and on the speaker as learner and communicator, looking at interactive aspects of communication.[31] Hinnenkamp's third phase of Gastarbeiterlinguistik is characterized by approaches that regard communication as a two-way activity needing to be analyzed in its social context, and later studies are more informed by social and anthropological theory and method, such as contrastive pragmatics and interpretive or interactional sociolinguistics, and often concentrate on intercultural aspects of communication (see, for instance, the papers in Auer and di Luzio 1984; and Hinnenkamp 1989).

Gastarbeiterdeutsch and the Determination of Ethnic Identity

In this brief—and necessarily selective—discussion, we have seen how the field of Gastarbeiterlinguistik has developed from one which was concerned primarily with the purely linguistic (formal) and universal characteristics of the way immigrants speak, to one which is concerned with social and intercultural interaction. What we have not yet pointed out are the repercussions of Gastarbeiterlinguistik for the immigrants themselves.

Hinnenkamp (1990:285) finds it remarkable that Gastarbeiterlinguistik developed as a subfield in the first place. He maintains that it is the only linguistic subdiscipline that is named after the object of its study. Even in sociolinguistics and variation studies in the United States, he says, where so much research has been carried out on African American dialects since the sixties, no one has ever proposed a subfield called "African American linguistics." Hinnenkamp maintains that there is no subfield called "feminist linguistics" or "worker linguistics," nor is there a subfield of German called "scientific German" or "legal German," even though these are recognizable concepts.[32] The only discipline that comes close to having a similar subfield, according to him, is *Ausländerpädagogik*, which like Gastarbeiterlinguistik indulges in the same process of what Hinnenkamp calls *Vereinna(h)mung* ("lumping together"/"naming together") of disparate entities.

Hinnenkamp's major complaint is that establishing a branch of linguistics tied to a social category prevented linguists from linking earlier with linguistic pragmatics, even though speech act theory and the contextual interpretation of speech acts were well known and well practiced in Germany from the seventies on. Moreover, he argues, this insistence on Gastarbeiterdeutsch meant that issues were ignored, such as the social and ethnic identity of the immigrants as groups and individuals. He maintains that this led, ironically albeit inadvertently, to the "ethnicization" of Gastarbeiter as a group and contributed to the groundswell of discrimination in German society:[33]

> Keinesfalls kann der "Gastarbeiter"-Status als Voraussetzung für diejenige Lernersprache gesehen werden, wie sie sich in der Beschreibung und Analyse des "Gastarbeiterdeutsch" niedergeschlagen hat. Die Subsumtion ganzer Kataloge linguistischer Defizite unter eine pan-ethnische und soziale Kategorie sowie die determinative Verbindung einer "defizitären" Varietät des Deutschen mit einer sozialen und pan-ethnischen Kategorie konnte den *Sonder-*

status dieser Kategorie nur verstärken. Denn von allen *möglichen* unterscheidbaren Kriterien gegenüber "Deutschen" hatte diese "Ethnisierbarkeit" längst den markantesten Distinktionsstatus zwischen "uns" und "denen" angenommen. Ethnizität wurde einerseits immer deutlicher "verwendbar" als *ausgrenzende Praxis* im alltäglichen Miteinander zwischen "Inländern" und "Ausländern" und andererseits immer deutlicher verwertbar als *erklärende Theorie* bei den beteiligten Wissenschaften.[34]

(Hinnenkamp 1990:286)

Hinnenkamp particularly blames interference theory for this ethnicization, which, while no longer regarding Gastarbeiterdeutsch as deficient, but only different, nevertheless puts the blame on the linguistic, cultural, and social background of the foreigners and still ignores the responsibility for interaction. Once again, this caused all the blame to be laid at the feet of the "ethnically other." Ethnicity was still not perceived as an interactional, dialogic process of identification, and German ethnic identity was again inadvertently reinforced by concentrating on what is different about *others* (288).

Indeed, Hinnenkamp's own studies show that this inadvertent separating out or ethnicization of Gastarbeiter is not reserved for linguists or educational scientists, but is common in everyday interactions between Germans and immigrants. One of his most telling examples is a contextual analysis of a bilingual Turkish-German street sign forbidding ball playing. The fact that in this street the prohibition was written in Turkish as well as in German, which is usually the accepted lingua franca amongst both Germans and Turks, is in itself an act of singling out Turks in a negative fashion. He suggests that, in general, information is given in Turkish when it is a question of a duty or obligation, but rarely when it is a matter of rights (291).[35] In a second study, Hinnenkamp (1982) analyzes an exchange between a German beggar and a foreign passerby. The passerby sympathizes with the plight of the beggar, but when the beggar realizes the passerby is a foreigner, he turns sour, probably in reaction to being categorized as a beggar by a Turk:

Bettler: Sie ham recht!
Passant: Es is nich gut.
Bettler: Nein, is nich gut.
Passant: Ja.
Bettler: Türkischmann Du?
Passant: Ja.
Bettler: Ich merk es.

Passant: Ja, muß man helfen, *aba + so.*
Bettler: *Sie brauchn mir nich helfen!*
Passant: Ja klar + ich meine + äähm ++ *wenn einer*
Bettler: (besonders schnell) *Sie ham=Sie ham recht!*[36]
(Hinnenkamp 1982, cited in Hinnenkamp 1990:292)

The linguistic behavior of the beggar here illustrates the position of the immigrant passerby. First, the beggar speaks to him in foreigner talk (*Türkischmann*, not *Türke*). Second, he addresses the passerby with the familiar and condescending *du*,[37] not the polite *Sie* form. Hinnenkamp also points out that the beggar's question carries the insinuation that the foreigner cannot even speak "proper" German. Feeling warranted in part by the interethnic character of this exchange, the beggar assumes the right to interrupt the passerby, to fob him off with stereotypical responses, and basically to ignore the interactional exchange between himself and his interlocutor.

All such types of behavior, whether exhibited by linguists, pedagogues, officials, or everyday people, serve to ethnicize both the minorities and, concomitantly, the Germans themselves. And language is the primary tool with which this ethnicization is achieved. What linguists—and others—need to bear in mind is the importance of understanding such processes as being made up of interactional, dialogic events.

Here, we return to Bourdieu's contention that the act of naming and classifying is a very strong exercise of power. This chapter has shown that classification struggles have been central in the field of Gastarbeiterlinguistik. In the beginning, linguists proceeded taxonomically in their treatment of the German of foreign workers, proceeding according to their training, their habitus. Much capital accrued to them from following the research trends of the time and developing a formalist, universalist view of foreign workers' language, which concentrated on linguistic forms per se and on those features that all languages have in common, regardless of the individual speaker. However, as time went on and as society changed, the field also moved on, recognizing that more attention must be paid to immigrants as a group of individuals, with each individual constrained in his or her performance by a unique constellation of social, political, economic, cultural, situational and linguistic factors. But the labels "Gastarbeiterdeutsch" and "Gastarbeiterlinguistik" have stuck, so that once again we are faced with a classic lag between naming conventions and the structure of society. The damage was clearly felt in the community: terms like "Gastarbeiterdeutsch" and "Pidgindeutsch" and "Gastarbeiterlinguistik," which have gained nationwide currency, serve to reinforce the difference between mainstream and nonmainstream groups. Comparing Gastarbeiter German with Standard German has also stacked the cards against foreign workers, begging the labels "inadequate," and, ultimately, "inferior." All of the labels have indirectly served to reinforce a stereotypical social reaction to foreign workers. These are terms that are imbued with negatives, and, in my opinion, it is time to shed them, in the way that the American linguistic community has constantly replaced terms that have become loaded with too many negative stereotypes (for example, "Non-Standard Negro English" and "Afro-American Vernacular English"). It is for this reason that I have used the neutral term "Foreign Worker German" rather than the expression "Gastarbeiterdeutsch."

In the next chapter we will see that at least one immigrant writer has objected expressly to the constraints imposed by the term "Gastarbeiterdeutsch," so that there is a direct link between the activities of the linguist and the nonlinguist. The fact is that the imposition of such labels has a negative impact on the foreign workers' quest for identity, regardless of whether they remain workers or aspire to other identities, such as "writer." We will take this issue of creating identity through language further, focusing our attention on literary activity in the immigrant community.

4. Language, Literature, and the Negotiation of Identity

Introduction

That immigrant groups profoundly influence the literature of their host country is attested by the works of Southeast European immigrants to the United States at the turn of the century, who embraced realism and naturalism and whose children (for example, Paul Gallico, Gregory Corso, and Mario Puzo) became the authors of the next generation. German immigrant workers have produced a body of literature in the last thirty years which has been dubbed, amongst other things, as *Gastarbeiterliteratur* ("guestworker literature"), *Migrantenliteratur* ("migrant literature"), *Ausländerliteratur* ("foreigner literature"), *Gastliteratur* ("guest literature"), or *Immigrantenliteratur* ("immigrant literature"). Indeed, the very naming of this literature is a controversial and deterministic act whose political, social, and literary ramifications we must consider in detail here.

Individual immigrant writers differ as to their choice of linguistic medium: some write in their native language and have their works translated into German; others write directly in German, choosing exclusively Standard German as their medium; still others code switch between Standard German and Foreign Worker German, sometimes interspersed with snatches of the home language. For some there is no choice of linguistic medium at all; for many the choice of medium is a conscious, not to say political, one; while for others the choice is simply a lifelike reflection of their naturally variable linguistic milieu. These choices, whether conscious or otherwise, are most revealing to those interested in the role of language and literary expression in society: they illustrate how language encodes linguistic attitudes as well as other essential human characteristics such as personal, group, and ethnic identity and social and political solidarity and ambitions; in short, the choice of linguistic medium helps us to understand the social relations and values a writer wishes to convey.

These topics are the subject matter of this chapter, in which we examine the role of language and literature in the negotiation of identity or identities for immigrants in the Federal Republic. The emergence of literary activity in the immigrant community naturally follows the socioeconomic and political history of postwar immigration, which we discussed in Chapter 1. It also follows the broad linguistic developments that were the subject matter of Chapter 3; here we explore the striking parallels between the linguistic and the literary situation.

The struggles of immigrant writers—first, for any voice at all with which to speak in a strange country; second, for recognition of their contributions as *literary* contributions; and, finally, for admission to the hallowed halls of *German* literature—distill the essential problems of the foreign workers in all spheres of activity in Germany. It cannot be surprising that the creative elite amongst the immigrants would be the ones to challenge prevailing conditions directly and strive overtly for change. Bourdieu (1977) has stressed the essential dialectic between objective social position (position in the class structure) and position in the classification struggle, that is, the struggle for capital. It falls to those in positions of relative power, in this case the intellectual elite, to wage a symbolic struggle which might ultimately improve the objective position of the group as a whole.

A Brief History of Literary Activity in the Immigrant Community[1]

The position of immigrant literature within (or *without*) modern German literature is currently a matter of considerable debate that once again illuminates German attitudes toward "Germanness" and "foreign-ness" and that illustrates the struggle between "us" and "them." In order to shed light on this controversy, we begin with a brief and selective history of literary activity in the immigrant community.

In the fifties, sixties, and early seventies there was almost no literary activity in the immigrant community. Aras Ören was an exception, probably since he chose to write his poetry in Turkish and publish it in German translation; even he, though, was known largely only in sociopolitically aware literary circles. On the whole, immigrant writers were constrained in this period by their personal situation, often isolated within national groups or stuck in literary ghettos (i.e., having a very restricted readership). However, as we will recall from Chapter 1, the seventies brought a change in immigration policy that permitted foreigners to settle in Germany, and this development forced them to get to grips with the German language as a medium for creative expression.

Between 1978 and 1980, four anthologies and eleven works of individual authors appeared in the Federal Republic and immigrant literature got its start, albeit largely ignored by the media and the commercial presses and heavily reliant on self-help groups and private initiatives. In 1980 immigrant writers founded the Polynationaler Literatur- und Kunstverein (PoLiKunst) and began publishing with the series *Südwind Gastarbeiterdeutsch*. PoLiKunst expressly promoted tolerance and mutual international understanding in all cultural domains and aimed to establish relationships between Germans and *kulturschaffende* ("culturally productive" foreigners; *Südwind Gastarbeiterdeutsch*, which was taken over by Neuer Malik Verlag (Kiel) in 1984, promulgated exclusively the works of writers from southern European countries. Other foreigner presses included Dagyeli Verlag (Frankfurt), Edition Cohn (Pulheim), and Verlag Atelier im Bauernhaus (Ottersberg), which generally published works in small editions. From such modest beginnings, the immigrant publications gradually gained a wider readership; today some of the larger paperback publishers such as Deutscher Taschenbuchverlag and Fischer and Rowohlt consistently publish immigrant literature.

The increase in publication reflects the literary recognition afforded immigrant-worker literature in the 1980s. In 1983 Suleman Taufiq was awarded the literature prize of the city of Aachen, and in 1984 Aysel Özakin was similarly honored by the Altona district of Hamburg. The Bavarian Academy of Fine Arts honored Aras Ören and the Italian writer Franco Biondi with its literary Förderpreis in 1983, and in 1985 these two shared the first ever Adalbert von Chamisso Prize, which has been awarded ever since in support of authors writing in German as a foreign language. The Turkish writer Saliha Scheinhardt was also awarded the literature prize of the town of Offenbach in 1985. Since that time, "guest worker literature" has been recognized as a salable commodity by German publishers; though, as we shall see, this does not come without its own price tag for immigrant writers and for the immigrant community as a whole.

While immigrant writers (or their parents, in the case of some second-generation writers) come from all over the world, Turks and Italians are the most prominent nationalities in immigrant-worker literature, not merely because the Turks represent the largest and most oppressed group[2] or because the Italians have been in Germany the longest. On the whole, they are much more active in the literary sense (and, as we shall see in the case of the Italians at least, often in the political sense) than the other groups. One of the major reasons why the Turks and Italians are more active than other ethnic groups is that they each represent a culture with its own very long literary tradition, at least in the middle and upper classes, and this tradition has filtered into the writing of the immigrants in the Federal Republic (Hamm 1988:32).

Although we have grouped Italians and Turks together, however, it must be pointed out that, on account of their very different history and status in Germany (and, indeed, within Europe), there are considerable differences between the two groups. As is typical of every ethnicity grouped together under the umbrella term "Gastarbeiter," Italians and Turks are united by the common features of their history as a group in Germany, and, at the same time, they are separated by those differences caused by contrasting features such as ethnic and cultural heritage and political status.

Italian Writers

The first great wave of postwar Italian immigrants came to Germany as a result of the recruitment agreement signed in 1955 (see Chapter 1). While the first Italian writers began working in the early 1960s, their work was largely inaccessible to the German public, as it was written in Italian, and it was of little interest to Italians in Italy, who were still completely ignorant of the plight of Italians in Germany.

In the late sixties, Italian writers in Germany finally gained a public audience with the help of the Italian information services, which sponsored competitions for Italian Gastarbeiter writers of poetry and prose. In the seventies, Italian language journals, and then bilingual journals, such as *Il Mulino* ("The Mill"), were published. In 1976 Franco Biondi's short story "Passavanti's Return" appeared in Italian in *Corriere della Sera* and, in 1982, the story was published in German translation (as "Passavantis Rückkehr"). The bilingual journal *Incontri* appeared in 1975, and in 1979 Biondi published a collection of poems entitled *Nicht nur gastarbeiterdeutsch*, marking the real beginning of the use of German as the language of immigrant-worker writers in Germany. The Italians thus led the way for all subsequent Gastarbeiter to follow. Biondi and Gino Chiellino write in German, while others, such as Carmine Abate and Vito d'Adamo, write in Italian and have their works translated into German.

That the Italians were leaders in these developments resulted partly from their sheer numerical representation and the length of their stay in Germany: by 1980 Germany had established itself as the most important target for Italian migration—hundreds of thousands had immigrated to Germany (863,232 between 1962 and 1976), with a huge percentage settling there permanently (Hamm 1988:38). Moreover, given the fact that they were the first nationality to be represented in conspicuous numbers in Germany, Italians were inevitably the first nationality to be the target of racism and nationalism after the economic crisis of 1966–67 (see Chapter 1). This discrimination was particularly severe in the early seventies, as attested by, for example, the explicitly anti-Italian racist outpourings of the television character Alfred Tetzlaff, the German equivalent of Alf Garnett in Britain or Archie Bunker in the United States. It is important to bear these facts in mind when considering the prominent literary-political activity of the Italian writers.

However, after the recruitment ban in November 1973, the legal position of the Italians in Germany changed, since as members of the EEC they (theoretically) enjoyed a more stable position than those immigrants from non-EEC countries. Consequently, Germans shifted their nationalist and racist attention to Yugoslavs and, particularly, to Turks, especially after the oil crisis of 1973. The Turks proved an easy target, since they gradually assumed the position of largest ethnic minority in Germany and since they were culturally, ethnically, and theologically much more distinct from the Germans than were the Italians and Yugoslavs. Chiellino (1985:40) points out that this shift of attention left the Italians in Germany in a precarious position, since they were supposed to consider themselves as EEC members in Germany, although technically they were still subject to the *Ausländergesetz* and were required to behave the way that German authorities dictated.

Reflecting their strong and long-standing socialist tradition, Italian writers in Germany are in general very sensitive to the difference between real and fake equality, not just with regard to themselves, but to all immigrants. They have been quick to point out that immigrants, especially non-EEC members, are highly underrepresented in all political spheres, from the national to the local level (although EEC members officially have the right to vote at the community *Gemeinde* level), and that they themselves are still subject to the strictures of the *Ausländergesetz*: "Die ausländerrechtlichen Sonderregelungen für EG-Staatsangehörige dürfen nicht darüber hinwegtäuschen, daß die Bundesrepublik wie auch die anderen Länder der Gemeinschaft, das Recht haben, Ausländer aus EG-Mitgliedsstaaten aus Gründen der 'öffentlichen Ordnung, der Sicherheit oder der Gesundheit' auszuweisen, bzw. ihnen den Aufenthalt zu verweigern."[3]

One major difference between Turks and Italians is thus clear and constitutes a difference that crosses other ethnic boundaries: immigrants from EEC countries are at least theoretically considered more secure than those who are not.

Turkish Writers

In general the Turks are regarded as the most vulnerable ethnic minority. Unlike the Italians, once the recruitment ban took place in 1973, the Turks suffered even greater prejudicial treatment from the native Germans. At this time they were by far the largest minority group in Germany, almost a million altogether; and, as we have seen, since that time their total number has almost doubled, owing not to new immigration, but to the arrival of asylum seekers and the unification of the families of workers already in Germany, as well as the subsequent birth of second-generation Turks.

The year 1973 also marks the beginning of Turkish Gastarbeiterliteratur: Nevzar Üstün, Bekir Yildiz, and Yüksel Pazarkaya had already published works in Turkish by the mid-sixties, many of which (for example, Üstün's *Almanya, Almanya* and Yildiz's *Die Türken in Deutschland*) had the consequences of Turkish migration to Germany as a theme. Pazarkaya is far and away the most prominent of these authors, since he has always written both in Turkish and in German and has thus always enjoyed a readership in both Turkey and Germany.[4] There followed in the seventies a number of stories and poems by a growing number of Turkish writers who, it must be said, had a hard time finding publishers for their works, but who did manage to communicate their experiences in literary form in newspapers and other journals (Hamm 1988:42). A number of Turkish writers joined the Gastarbeiter in Germany in the seventies receiving political asylum from the German government after fleeing from the extremists and, later, from the military regime in Turkey. One of the most successful writers in asylum in Germany was Fakir Baykurt who wrote in Turkish but had his works translated and published in German. Aras Ören is among the most important Turkish writers in Germany today. A number of his anthologies have enjoyed great success, and Ören is certainly the most prolific Turkish writer. As we noted above, he received a literature prize from the Bavarian Academy of Fine Arts and shared the Adalbert von Chamisso Prize with Franco Biondi.

Other Turkish writers to be mentioned here are Günay Dal, Adalet Agaoglu, and Aysel Özakin. Özakin is notable for the fact that after having her first published works translated into German, her poetry collection *Du bist willkommen* was written directly in German. More and more Turks followed her lead and wrote in German, particularly those of the second generation (Levent Aktoprak, Akif Pirinçci, Ihsan Atacan, Zafer Senoçak, Zehra Çirak). Many of these younger writers moved to the Federal Republic at an early age or were born in Germany and, indeed, learned German even more readily than they learned Turkish. Two other Turkish authors are distinguished for the fact that they write exclusively in German, namely, Sinasi Dikmen, the satirist and cabaret artist, and Saliha Scheinhardt, the female writer.

Turkish immigrant literature developed quite differently from the Italian and is marked primarily by its relatively apolitical character (though not all writers, notably Pazarkaya, would regard themselves as apolitical). A number of the Turkish writers see themselves by no means as Gastarbeiter authors, but rather as Turks. Ören, Pazarkaya, Özakin, and Dal, for example, have kept a critical distance from political groups such as PoLiKunst and have little or no multicultural or multinational interest (Hamm 1988:45-46). Nor has the difference between the Italians and Turks come about by accident: many of the Turkish writers were already writers in Turkey before they came to Germany. Although they themselves took up the theme of Gastarbeiter, they could consider themselves as workers in the way that the Italians saw themselves.

Moreover, the political position of the Turks is radically different from that of the Italians, as we have mentioned. Turks are not (yet) EEC members and, not having the same freedom of movement and occupation as the Italians, are much more susceptible to the caprices of the *Ausländergesetz*. The Turks (particularly the Kurds) are even subject to scrutiny by the authorities in their own country, who can withdraw their rights to renew their passports in the face of perceived negative political activity (Hamm 1988:46-47). For these reasons it is hardly surprising that their political profile is not as high as that of the Italians.

Other Nationalities; Men and Women; Other Types of Foreigner

While we have concentrated here on Turks and Italians, we must recognize that many other nationalities are represented amongst immigrant writers, if not in the same numbers as those from Turkey and Italy. We should mention, at least, the prolific, best-selling author from Syria, Rafik Schami, and his countrymen Suleman Taufiq and Adel Karasholi (who immigrated originally to the former GDR), as well as the poet SAID from Iran, and the Lebanese writer Jusuf Naoum. There is, moreover, a broad spectrum of nationalities among women writers, among which there is a significant number of Turkish writers, including Saliha Scheinhardt, Zehra Çırak, Alev Tekinay, and Melek Baklan. Though Italian women are practically unrepresented, there are several productive women writers from Eastern Europe, such as Vera Kamenko, Irena Vrkljan, and Dragica Rajcic (the former Yugoslavia), Rumjana Zacharieva (Bulgaria), Zsuzsanna Gahse (Hungary), and Libuse Monikova (the former Czechoslovakia). Other active and successful immigrant women writers worth mentioning are Torkan (Iran), Eleni Torossi and Fotini Ladaki (Greece), as well as a number of Asian writers, such as Hisako Matsubara and Yoko Tawada (Japan) and Kim Lan Thai (Vietnam).[5] Amongst the best known Asian male writers is the Tuvin national Galsan Tschinag, who won the Adalbert von Chamisso Prize in 1992.

It cannot be stressed often enough that not all of these immigrant writers can be classified as writers of Gastarbeiterliteratur or, indeed, as ever having anything to do with Gastarbeiter. To take just two examples, Libuse Monikova has always counted as an intellectual and has held a number of university positions. Galsan Tschinag was never a long-term immigrant; he went to Germany as a student, studied in Leipzig, and in fact wrote a number of his works in German after he left Germany. Monikova would be better subsumed under the heading of immigrant literature, and Tschinag under the heading of foreigner literature. What all these writers do share is the immigrant experience, however impermanent, though this by no means dictates that they should engage this experience in their work.

Common Themes of Immigrant Literature

While one should be cautious about trying to bring such a large and disparate body of works and writers together under any label, it is nevertheless the case, at least in "traditional" Gastarbeiterliteratur, that common themes emerged naturally out of the shared experience as immigrants in an industrial society. Franco Biondi observes three theme complexes in traditional immigrant ("emigrant" in his usage) literature, which I have interpreted as follows:

1. the first confrontation with emigrant existence (leaving family and friends and one's familiar surroundings; the first journey abroad, facing the reality of one's destination, the actual arrival, language difficulties, bureaucratic problems, etc.).
2. the immigrant experience (life in the new country: living, working, the confrontation with a different culture, different customs; alienation, homesickness and the longing for familiar surroundings, memories of the home village, discrimination, complaints about abuse, civil rights, everyday experiences, current political events in the home country).

3. so-called free topics (particular events in the family, e.g., the marriage of a daughter, the birth of a child, etc.; existential questions, so-called free themes; nature, natural disasters, trivial themes such as parodies of pop song lyrics, etc.).

(1984:87)

A major function of the first phase of immigrant literature was to document immigrants' treatment, their feelings, and their culture shock: "ihre Irritation in der neuen, fremden Umgebung, ihre Begegnung mit einer fremden Gesellschaft und Kultur, mit ungewohnten und oft ungekannten Produktionsmitteln und -verhältnissen, ihr Heimweh, ihre Sehnsüchte und Hoffnungen, ihre neuen Leiden und Freuden"[6] (Yüksel Pazarkaya, quoted in Kreuzer 1984:103). But perhaps that literature's most important function was to give the immigrants a voice and a conversation partner: "die Isolation in der Fremde durch Schreiben zu füllen . . . oder . . . ein Zeugnis über die eigene Lebenschronik abzulegen, bzw. diese mitzuteilen"[7] (Biondi 1984:87). This phase of writing is characterized by highly personal and unskilled essays and poems, written by lonely workers who needed to pour their desperate isolation onto paper in their native language:

> Die Sprache, die gegen diese Isolation eingesetzt wird, ist die Sprache der unmittelbaren Umgebung. Eine Umgebung, die von den mitgebrachten Erinnerungen genauso stark geprägt ist, wie vom Alltag in der Fremde. Diese Sprache kann sowohl der Dialekt des Heimatdorfes sein, häufig aber ist es ein sehr wenig anspruchsvolles Italienisch. Ort des Schreibens, ein Zimmer im Wohnheim, in einer Werkswohnung, ein Zimmer in der Stadt, wo man eben alleine lebt.[8]
>
> (Gino Chiellino 1985:31, cited in Hamm 1988:33)

Once the recruitment ban took place and immigrants realized they were going to stay, they began to write in German. The German language became a means of increasing their audience, of confronting the Germans, and of uniting against their common plight. German was seen as a way for foreigners of different backgrounds to communicate with one another and form a community. Hamm saw the use of German and with it the development of German-language Gastarbeiterliteratur as a move toward the "solidarization of all guest workers" (1988:35). Raddatz sees this early work as a kind of "literature of the working world," which manifested the shock of living in a foreign land in the form of diaries, almanacs, first anthologies and publications in the smallest publishing houses (1994:45).

Without a doubt this quest for identity was simultaneously a quest for capital, both symbolic cultural capital and more tangibly economic capital, to borrow Bourdieu's terms. At this stage in their development, immigrant writers were willing to sacrifice individual identity to group concerns and occupational expedience—especially as this seemed to be opening the doors of publishing houses to them. To these writers, publishing was a way to negotiate an identity and to find a voice.

As immigrants ventured to write more and more in German, their work included topics that reflected their new challenges in German society: integration, assimilation, confrontation with the new culture, *Ausländerfeindlichkeit*:

> Die Emigranten, die sich entschlossen haben, in Deutschland zu bleiben, sahen sich ebenfalls mit zahlreichen Problemen konfrontiert. Das Phänomen der Emigration wurde komplexer. Es verlor mehr und mehr den Charakter der Vorläufigkeit und Themen der Anfangsjahre wie die des Heimwehs büßten an ihrer vorherrschenden Stellung ein. Das Leben in der neuen Heimat bedeutete gleichzeitig eine Auseinandersetzung mit einer anderen Kultur. Daß sich dieses Problem nicht leicht lösen ließ, zeigte sich daran, daß schon bald der Ruf nach dem Sprung über die Gettomauer laut wurde.[9]
>
> (Biondi 1984:80)

While the common themes of immigrant writers might have been enough to bind (many of) them together under the term Gastarbeiter at this stage, the form and style of their work, which mirrored incipient abilities in both language and creative production, were not yet of a standard to be universally considered Gastarbeiter*literatur*. This opinion is represented in the following remarks by Raddatz:

> Das ist wohl die Phase, in der man in Gedichten von Biondi von "Krümmeln" statt Krümeln, von einer "runtergehenden Sonne" lesen kann oder die Konstruktion "als wie es normal sei" findet statt "als ob es normal sei." Es ist zugleich die Phase, in der Kemal Kurt sich wehmütig mit kleinen Prosaskizzen an den heimatlichen türkischen Klatschmohnsirup, die Hochzeiten oder den Melonenmost erinnert—Wehmutsfetzen der Verschlagenen, berührend, naiv. Literatur ist das nicht.[10]
>
> (1994:45)

On the other hand, a number of academics, particularly Harald Weinrich and Irmgard Ackermann of the Institut für Deutsch als Fremdsprache of the University of Munich, which stimulated the creative activity of foreigners in German with its Adalbert von Chamisso Prize, were quick to appreciate a special kind of linguistic creativity in this early work. Specifically, Weinrich draws parallels with the Russian Formalists who considered writing to be poetic only when it drew the reader's attention to the language itself and prevented them from getting through the text too quickly. Biondi's poem "nicht nur gastarbeiterdeutsch," which we discuss below, is an excellent example of what Weinrich is talking about here.

During this period, language itself was thematized in the literary works. Writers and poets wrote about Gastarbeiterdeutsch, often in Gastarbeiterdeutsch, and, while their major thrust was no doubt its societal function, they still managed to provide a number of direct and indirect comments on its form. Indeed, language is treated as an integral part of all of the problems facing immigrants, and language, or the lack of it, becomes a central theme around which discussions of identity turn.

The literature that was written solely in German in the early stages was generally more remarkable for its content than its form. The reasons for the lack of literary form were straightforward: the immigrants had neither the knowledge of German language, nor of German literature, to produce literature that could compare with mainstream German works. Seibert discusses Biondi's explanation of the form issue as follows (Biondi was writing under the pseudonym Liverani 1982:11–14):

> Die Vernachlässigung von Formfragen gegenüber Fragen des Inhalts entspräche—so in Liveranis Vorwort—zudem den Lebensbedingungen der Arbeitsmigration: die Gastarbeiterliteratur "kann sich nicht aufgrund der gegebenen Wirklichkeit des Emigrantendaseins auf linguistische Feinheiten, auf die Form stützen. . . ." Eine solche als notwendig behauptete augenblickliche Marginalisierung ästhetischer Probleme ist also Resultat und gleichzeitig auch Indiz für die Authentizität dieser Literatur. . . . Daß die *Betroffenen* sich hier äußern würden, wird immer wieder betont; Liverani schließt sein Vorwort mit dem Hinweis, "gemeinsam" sei den Gedichten, "daß sie echt erlebt sind und direkt aus der eigenen Haut herauskommen."[11]
>
> (1984:47)

In other words, infelicities of form add to the authenticity of the literature.

Biondi pointed out already in December 1976 that it made no sense to judge this new genre of literature using classical criteria, since the authors had other aims entirely. Instead, he argued, the aesthetic categories need to be tailored both to the special relationship between content and form in immigrant literature and to the basic preconditions of the immigrants ("emigrants") themselves (Biondi 1984:83).

Negotiating Labels

Perhaps nowhere is the struggle for identity in the immigrant population so clearly manifested as in the negotiation of a label for their writing. Once again, within the academic community, a major preoccupation has been the naming (and fixing) of the genre. But just as writers and critics have been unable to agree on a uniform set of criteria for judging immigrant literature as literature, they have also been unable to find a satisfactory umbrella term for it. The label "Gastarbeiterliteratur" is a controversial one, partly because it has become loaded with negative connotations, as has the word "Gastarbeiterdeutsch," which was discussed in Chapter 3, and partly because of the fact that not every immigrant writer is or ever has been a Gast*arbeiter*. Harald Weinrich used the term "Gastliteratur" earlier on, which expressly omits the *Arbeiter* ("worker") element, then later he also used "Ausländerliteratur," since for him this latter subsumes the asylum seekers, the repatriated Aussiedler, and foreign academics and students, as well as the workers themselves who write within this genre. Others, such as Schierloh (1984) and Horn (1986), propose the term "Migrantenliteratur," arguing that it subsumes the process of migration so fundamental to the genre. In many respects these difficulties mirror the difficulties one has in naming the immigrant groups themselves, which we discussed in the Introduction.

Echoing Bourdieu, Fairclough (1989) has pointed out the drawbacks of linguistic determinism. With the terms used in German for foreigner literature, we have a clear example of classification placing limitations on behavior. Ackermann points out that the term "Ausländerliteratur" brings with it a certain set of expectations that are ultimately constraining to non-German writers. While in the beginning, the term "Gastarbeiterliteratur" was even used by some of the writers themselves, it has become inaccurate and misleading and, "by using a sociologically disputed term, leads above all to marginalization which is neither acceptable for those affected by it, nor helpful toward creating understanding among others" (1991:1). This is a crucial point, to which we will return later in this chapter.

As an alternative to these terms, which were largely imposed from above, some of the actual authors coined the terms *authentische Liter-*

atur[12] ("authentic literature") and *Literatur der Betroffenheit*[13] ("affected literature"). These labels were devised in part as a response to the criticism that not all writers are true Gastarbeiter. It was argued that all of the writers had shared the experience of immigration to a foreign land and that all had been affected by it. Moreover, it must be stressed that, while many successful immigrant writers have achieved above-average educational and social status, the vast majority of first-generation authors have nevertheless actually lived as Gastarbeiter, for varying lengths of time. For instance, Franco Biondi went to Germany in 1967 with his family and worked as a mechanic, welder, chemical industry worker, and production worker for ten years. He went to school part-time, gaining his school certificates and his *Abitur*, and then studied psychology. He now earns his living both as an author and psychologist. Jusuf Naoum worked in the hotel trade for a number of years and then worked as a masseur and hydrotherapist until 1983, when he was able to make a living as a freelance writer. Rafik Schami also held various jobs after moving to Germany in 1971, before getting his Ph.D. in 1979, and Saliha Scheinhardt worked for years as a sewing machinist in a textile factory before gaining her academic qualifications and developing a career as a writer (Hamm 1988:50). These, and the many other similar biographies prominently placed on the covers of many published works by immigrants, attest to the writers' "authentic" past as Gastarbeiter.

According to Hamm, the same holds true for writers of the second generation. They either came to Germany with their parents or were born there, and experienced the everyday life of a Gastarbeiter for years as they were growing up, leaving the ranks of the common Gastarbeiter only upon gaining their *Abitur* or degree. Both first- and second-generation writers have a crucial distance from their past that allows them to deal with the everyday life of the Gastarbeiter in their writing. This distance helps to insulate the author from the trials and tribulations of being a Gastarbeiter in Germany and allows him/her at one and the same time to identify with the immigrants, but preserve a certain distance from them. Hamm argues that this *Betroffenheit* of the writers places Gastarbeiterliteratur within the German literary framework of the seventies—the umbrella literary genre *Neue Subjektivität*, in which the writer is in general at the center of the work (I), and autobiographical literature (of the "I was there" sort)—that took the place of the documentary, biographical *Neue Sachlichkeit* of the 1960s. For Hamm, women's literature of the seventies is comparable to the Gastarbeiterliteratur of the eighties, and this confirms the collapse of German literature into *Gruppenliteratur*. Like women's writing, (early)

Gastarbeiterliteratur represents an underprivileged group which is voicing its *Betroffenheit* and trying through it to find community and communication: "Die Betroffenheit, die so zum Ausdruck kommt, ist das Bindeglied der Gruppe: Betroffen sind Türken, Italiener, Griechen oder Spanier gleichermaßen. Die gemeinsame Betroffenheit sichert den Gastarbeiterautoren Geschlossenheit"[14] (Hamm 1988:51).

All active fields move on, however; in more recent discussions of immigrant literature, the notion of authenticity is played down and sometimes directly lamented by the writers themselves. For example, in discussing the reception of Franco Biondi's 1991 novel *Die Unversöhnlichen—Im Labyrinth der Herkunft*, Rafik Schami expressly wishes that discussions could get beyond "[d]as alte Besprechungsthema auf der Basis erlebter Authentizität, wonach jeder ausländische Schriftsteller als Autor ein Gastarbeiter sein muß, der alles persönlich erlebt hat und deswegen zum Schriftsteller geworden ist"[15] (1991:237).

Apart from the fact that some of these writers have never been Gastarbeiter, a considerable number do not write about "typical immigrant themes." The question, therefore, is raised of whether these writers should be classified under the same rubric as others who do address such themes. The label "Ausländerliteratur" is so all-consuming that a number of non-German writers of German-language literature in Germany have striven to distance themselves from the Gastarbeiter image from the outset. Ota Filip, SAID, Zsuzsanna Gahse, and Libuse Monikova[16] avoid these topics "on principle" (Ackermann 1991:1). Others, including Rafik Schami and Gino Chiellino, who were directly involved in setting the literary program for immigrant writers in the beginning, also touch upon these topics only in some of their works. In fact, most of the writers now feel overly constrained by the expectations of the presses and their reading public. Though Hamm (1988:30) argues that, when it comes to publishing, "Der Makel 'Gastarbeiter' ist hier von Vorteil,"[17] Gino Chiellino (quoted in Raddatz 1994:45) warns of its grave disadvantages to writers viewed not as individuals, but as a collective sociological "phenomenon," echoing those remarks of Hinnenkamp quoted at the end of Chapter 3. Linking *Betroffenheit* with Gastarbeiterdeutsch is seen as a hindrance to the literary endeavor, preventing immigrant writing from developing beyond the level of a linguistic curiosity and a social cause. The label has degenerated from a positive marker of group identity for the authors to a stigma. There is a clear shift here in the distribution of capital, both economic and symbolic, and, while the publishing houses insist on *Betroffenheit*, Gastarbeiterdeutsch, and *Gastarbeiterthematik*, their function has become a kind of literary straitjacket for their former proponents: "Die unglückliche Verbindung von 'Gastarbeiterdeutsch' und 'Betroffenheit' hat dazu geführt, daß kaum eine kritische Arbeit über diese Literatur vorhanden ist, die sich die Mühe gemacht hätte, sie zum Gegenstand von Literaturkritik zu machen. Sie wird weiterhin von den Literaturkritikern als ein Zwitter verstanden, der die Sprach- und Sozialforscher angeht"[18] (45).

It is at this crucial moment that the historical and the linguistic and the literary aspects of being a foreigner all come together. If we doubted the impact of linguistic determinism in the last chapter, surely its direct force must be admitted now.

Perhaps the most pertinent reason for rejecting such alienating terms as "Ausländerliteratur" is that many of the authors involved have lived so long and worked so long in Germany and contributed so much and become so integrated into the German literary scene that they can no longer be considered "foreigners" in any real sense: "Wieviel Unverschämtheit gehört eigentlich dazu, 'Ausländer-Literatur' zu nennen, was integraler Bestandteil unserer Lyrik, Prosa, Satire ist? Wieviel staunenden Respekt vielmehr haben wir zu zollen diesen Schriftstellern, die souverän, spielerisch und gelegentlich nahezu genial mit der deutschen Sprache arbeiten—einige von ihnen (wie Rafik Schami) bereits Bestsellerautoren"[19] (Raddatz 1994:45).

What we need to understand here is that—as we saw with Foreign Worker German in the last chapter—there is no one monolithic entity Gastarbeiterliteratur; the field has moved on, just as society has moved on in Germany. We shall need to consider further the question of the literary position of German (language) literature written by nonnative speakers, but first we need to turn our attention to the role of language in immigrant literature.

The Role of Language in the Negotiation of Ethnic and Social Identity

What emerges from the discussion to this point is that immigrant authors are now clamoring for a change of label and of identity. Whereas some were content at first to identify with Gastarbeiter, they now recognize the social and professional constraints this identity places on them. The search for identity is a theme that has always been of primary importance in immigrant (if not in all contemporary) literature, and its nature has changed along with other historical developments. In order to understand its most recent manifestations and their implications, we need to consider the theme's progression from its original form.

Rather than take a philosophical approach to identity, I espouse a social-psychological interpretation, according to which identity is not a fixed and/or ascribed property of an individual, but is rather acquired and negotiated in intercourse with other individuals and is therefore subject to change, imposition, and even destruction by others. I therefore also regard it not as a stable and inalienable possession of the individual, but rather as a variable and dynamic phenomenon that can change across time and in response to any number of social and environmental factors. In particular, I hold with Goffman (1955) that identity can be negotiated in face-to-face interaction and that this negotiation of identity is especially salient exactly where it is challenged.

Any discussion of identity for immigrants has to be linked with the notion of ethnicity, which itself is a difficult concept to define. Most commentators, for example, Edwards (1985) and Breton and Pinard (1960), point to the fundamentally involuntary nature of ethnicity: "we might tentatively view ethnicity as an involuntary state in which members share common socialization practices or culture" (Edwards 1985:8). But if ethnicity is an "accident of birth," then we must agree with Edwards that it is difficult to comprehend how ethnicity persists across the generations, given that society is subject to rapid and profound change. For Edwards, even in the absence of specific cultural content, "a sense of 'groupness' may persist long after visible or tangible links with earlier generations have disappeared" (8). It appears that neither nativity, a shared language, nor a sense of nation is necessary or sufficient for a group to experience the sort of belonging we understand by the term ethnicity. What appears to be most important is a feeling of groupness.

Shibutani and Kwan define an ethnic group as consisting of people who perceive of themselves as being "of a kind . . . united by emotional bonds"; although they may share a common heritage, "far more important . . . is their belief that they are of a common descent" (1965: 40–41). Edwards stresses the fact that ethnic identity can be presumed by citing Weber (1968): "We shall call 'ethnic groups' those that entertain a subjective belief in their common descent. . . . it does not matter whether or not an objective blood relationship exists. Ethnic membership . . . differs from the kinship group precisely by being a *presumed* identity" (1985:389; Edwards's italics). Edwards himself also regards ethnicity as a "matter of belief" (389).

The implications of this discussion for the immigrant workers in Germany are significant. By being born in other countries or by being born to foreign or once-foreign parents, immigrant workers constitute a group that is different and separate from other groups in Germany. The difference is in the immigration experience and also in the variant culture, values, *Weltanschauung*, sense of group identity, and linguistic history, if not necessarily in linguistic ability. On the one hand, these properties are relatable to the (comparatively) uncontroversial and established ethnicities of an individual's forebears: Turkish, Greek, Yugoslav, Portuguese, etc. On the other, the designations "Gastarbeiter" and "foreign worker" significantly apply not only to those who are, in fact, first-generation immigrants, but also to their offspring and their offspring's offspring, who might even hold a German passport.[20] "Gastarbeiter" denotes a group that may or may not have been born in Germany, but that is certainly regarded as not belonging to mainstream German society. It denotes a group with "common socialization practices and culture" in the sense that they are also not consonant with mainstream German practices and culture, and it also unites this group, stressing emotional bonds and a "heritage" that encompasses common experiences in the *Gastland*. In other words, it would appear that ethnic identity as Turk, Greek, Italian, etc. persists within the local group, while these indentities in contrast to the larger group of mainstream Germans are subsumed under the generic, non-German ethnicity of "Gastarbeiter." The term is more than just an ethnic denominator, it is a social denominator, classifying immigrants as members of a particular class *plus* ethnic type. Although it is an oppositional term, the pertinent oppositions can vary according to both the specific social situation and the point of view of its user.

Whether or not we consider it feasible to regard the immigrant workers as a new ethnicity or ethnosocial group, we cannot deny the importance of the fact that by their segregation from mainstream Germans they do in various ways display different group boundaries, that they are indeed part of a different group to which many express overt allegiance largely because of their shared history:

> Ethnic identity is allegiance to a group—large or small, socially dominant or subordinate—with which one has ancestral links. There is no necessity for a continuation, over generations, of the same socialization or cultural patterns, but some sense of a group boundary must persist. This can be sustained by shared objective characteristics (language, religion, etc.), or by more subjective contributions to a sense of "groupness," or by some combination of both. Symbolic or subjective attachments must relate, at however distant a remove, to an observably real past.
>
> (Edwards 1985:10)

The "real past" of the Gastarbeiter is their immigration history and their experiences in the *Gastland*. Early immigrant-worker literature suggests that many immigrant workers have designated themselves as "Gastarbeiter," and that this identity transcends their original nationality.

What is symbolic of the Gastarbeiter as a whole is the stereotypical variety of German that can be simulated by lay Germans and that, on this superficial level, displays remarkable uniformity, regardless of the first-language background of the individual speakers or their parents. Perhaps it is this symbolic Gastarbeiterdeutsch which unites the immigrant workers most closely, both in the eyes of the mainstream Germans and within the group, since it affords them the opportunity to communicate on a universal level, and in so doing inevitably promotes unity as a group. Edwards has suggested that "many have considered the possession of a given language as well-nigh essential to the maintenance of group identity" (1985:3) and that "to the extent to which language remains as a valued symbolic feature of group life, it may yet contribute to the maintenance of boundaries" (7). Whether one accepts the stronger position, that immigrant workers and their descendants constitute a new ethnicity in Germany, or whether one prefers the weaker view, that they possess a separate identity as a differentiated group of people, one cannot deny the role of language in the maintenance of this separateness. It is remarkable that superficially minute linguistic details can serve as such strong symbols separating Germans from foreign workers and one subgroup of immigrant workers from another. In defining the term "ethnicity," Edwards (1985:7) calls upon the work of Barth (1969), who stresses the importance of emphasizing *group boundaries* or *group content*. For Barth, the boundaries between groups are what is essential in maintaining ethnic differences, since they can be maintained long after the group itself has changed. Despite the fact that we are now seeing the second and third generation born to immigrant workers, that is to say, children and grandchildren being born in Germany, their "ethnic" designation as Gastarbeiter or *Gastarbeiterkind* is maintained. This will remain the case so long as there is sensitivity to the group boundary, which manifests itself within the linguistic substratum effect and elsewhere. Attention to these linguistic details provides a key to understanding the literature of the group, as well as the prevailing social relations between foreigners and the mainstream in the Federal Republic.

Language, Lack of Language, and Multilingualism

In German immigrant literature, many works that deal with identity revolve around the split personality of the first generation and the general lack of identity of the second. That this is indeed *a* (if not *the*) most prominent theme in the literature is attested by the fact that a large number of first-generation writers directly confront their split identity in writing, as when Hasan Dwran describes himself as having one arm in Anatolia and one arm in Germany ("Was wird aus uns?" in Ney 1984:139).

Writers emphasize their position in a sort of "no-man's-land" where they feel themselves to be neither flesh nor fowl, or "Bach" or "doner kebab," as Aysel Özakin (1985:16) puts it. The following passage by HSM[21] illustrates this in general terms: "In keiner Gesellschaft werden wir akzeptiert. In der BRD sind wir Gastarbeiter, Ausländer, noch schlimmer: die Türken. In den Heimatländern sind wir Deutschländer, die Alemannen, noch schlimmer: die Kapitalisten"[22] (quoted in Ackerman 1984b:14). Anna Christina de Jesus Dias described it as the dilemma of choosing between being a stranger in a strange land or a stranger at home: "In Deutschland war ich eine Ausländerin und in Portugal war ich 'die Deutsche.' Wohin gehöre ich?"[23] (quoted in Ackermann 1984b:23). Many of the writers feel they are split between two countries; particularly in "travel pieces," where they commute between Germany and their home country, the dual life and their contradictory identities are manifest:

ANGORA

Ankara
Mir fremd
doch nah

Aus deinen Armen bin ich rausgewachsen
Gleich hast du
mich wieder
und ich
werde dich begrüßen
Zwischen uns
lebt
offen und verborgen
mehr als nur
ein Leben[24]

(Levent Aktoprak 1987, *Unterm Arm die Odysee*)

Consideration of the language issue brings us to the heart of the identity crisis that pervades much of the writing that belongs to immigrant literature, whether it be written by the first or the second generation. Indeed, language is an integral part of all of the problems facing immigrants, and it takes a central place in many works: "Wir reden gemischt, weder richtig Deutsch, noch richtig Türkisch, Italienisch oder Griechisch. Wir sind in keiner Sprache mehr zuhaus. Wir sind auf der vergeblichen Suche nach einer Antwort auf die Frage, wer wir eigentlich sind"[25] (HSM, quoted in Ackermann 1984b:19). As Hamm puts it: "Sprache wird zum Kristallisationspunkt. Sie ist vielen schreibenden Ausländern ein Symbol ihrer kulturellen Unzugehörigkeit.... Sprache, genauer: mangelhafte sprachliche Ausdrucksfähigkeit wird zum Träger ethnischer und kultureller Identitätsschwierigkeit"[26] (1988:99).

This awareness of the importance of language is reflected in the literature which self-consciously discusses it:

> Bevor ich ein Wort spreche aus
> nachdenke ich gründlich darüber
> Mir soll laufen unter kein Fehler
> damit ich nicht falle auf
> vor einem so erlesenen Publikum
> als unkundiger Trottel
> der sich benimmt immer daneben[27]
> (Ivan Tapia Bravo, quoted in Ackermann 1984b:233)

A number of writers use their imperfect bilingualism as an often painful emblem of their indeterminate status and their indeterminate identity:

> Du lebst in zwei Sprachen,
> Doch du beherrscht keine.
> Die eine verlernst du,
> Du mißbrauchst die andere.[28]
>
> Tu habites deux langues
> Mais tu n'en possèdes aucune.
> Pour ce qui est de l'une
> Tu l'oublies,
> L'autre tu l'écorches.
> (Chantal Estran-Goecke, quoted in Ackermann 1984b:80)

SPRACHFELDER

> In meinem Kopf haben sich
> die Grenzen zweier Sprachen
> verwischt
> doch
> zwischen mir
> und mir
> verläuft noch

der Trennzaun
der Wunden zurückläßt
jedesmal
wenn ich ihn öffne[29]
(Franco Biondi, quoted in Ackermann 1984b:104).

Some of the first-generation immigrants directly politicize the question of their identity, as does Franco Biondi in the following piece, which expressly addresses the exploitation of Gastarbeiter as an expendable resource:

Und auf meiner Stirn, auf meiner Jacke stand seit Geburt geschrieben: Gastarbeiter; das bedeutete: ausbeutbar, rechtlos, abschiebbar. Mit diesem Wort wurde mit Stempel und Siegel das Schicksal besiegelt. Und dieses Wort hatte jemand für uns erfunden und geschrieben, jemand, der uns nicht kannte, der den Gewinn aus diesem Wort abschätzen konnte und auch Gewinn machte.[30]
("Und nun schieben sie uns ab," in Biondi et al. 1980:142)

Franco Biondi and Rafik Schami (1983) attack the propensity of native Germans to lump all the Gastarbeiter together with the ironic slogan: *Ein Gastarbeiter ist ein Türke*. There is a delicious contradiction in a slogan like this: on the one hand, it has a solidarity appeal to all foreign workers; on the other, it expresses contempt for the *Vereinna(h)mung* (Hinnenkamp 1990) of all foreigners *by others*. Such literary insights serve as historical documentation, mirroring the changes in attitude of societal groups; on this basis, many writers use their work directly to attack the status quo and agitate for change and improvement (see Hamm 1988:113).

Citing Birol Denizeri, Hamm (1988) points out that language can act as a weapon: "Ich ging zu Euch, ihr sagtet, lerne zuerst Deutsch. Ich lernte Deutsch, ging wieder zu Euch. Ihr machtet mich mit den Perversionen Eurer Sprache bekannt, mit Türkenwitzen"[31] (Birol Denizeri in Ackermann 1984a:69). Hamm regards language as another tool used by the Germans to control the Gastarbeiter. But German can also be exploited by the immigrants themselves as a means of communicating and thus of helping each other, reducing isolation, impotence, and anonymity. In this sense, the use of the German language by Gastarbeiter can be regarded as "a step toward solidarity, a sign of growing power in a situation of powerlessness" (115):

[Die Literatur der Gastarbeiter] soll vielmehr die ansprechen, die mit Gastarbeitern auf derselben Ebene stehen, aber auch die, die von ihrer Situation, wie sie noch ist und werden kann, erfahren wollen, damit sie sie besser verstehen. Hierbei wird versucht, die literarische Kommunikation zunehmend in Deutsch zu schreiben. Damit wollte und will man das Gemeinsame betonen, um Brücken zu schlagen zu den deutschen Mitbürgern und zu den verschiedensten Minderheiten anderer Sprachherkunft in der Bundesrepublik.[32]

(Biondi and Schami 1981:134)

Ethnically Marked Linguistic Variants[33]

Apart from seeing language as an overall concept playing a role in the struggle for identity, we must recognize the symbolic function of ethnically marked varieties of Foreign Worker German in creating and contrasting different identities. As a remarkable echo of linguists' search for universal features of Foreign Worker German, a "generic" variety of Foreign Worker German appears in literature that serves to neutralize ethnic differences and unite all foreign workers and their families into one group with perceived common characteristics. However, at the same time, perceptible and significant subdivisions within this group can be reflected in surface differences in the language invoked by a writer when he or she wishes to contrast foreign worker with foreign worker, as opposed to foreign worker with mainstream German. Thus the linguistic tokens characteristic of Gastarbeiterdeutsch fulfill two complementary roles: when individualizing characteristics are neutralized, they serve to unite all foreign workers against the mainstream Germans; when differences are stressed, they bring into sharper relief the individual ethnicities that make up the umbrella group. Thus these differences function concurrently as stereotypical tokens of a specific group's identity and as markers of varying in-group and out-group relations amongst the foreigners and mainstream Germans; that is, they signal dynamic, multiple, and sometimes even contradictory identities.

Discussing Giles (1979), Marianne Saville-Troike (1989) points out that a speech community consisting of multiple ethnic groups may display various patterns of language use:

(1) subgroups in the community may use only their minority ethnic language(s);
(2) minority group members may be bilingual in their ethnic language(s) and the dominant language; or
(3) minority group members may be monolingual in the dominant language.

Where conditions (1) and (2) obtain, she says, "members of minority groups who identify themselves as such often speak a distinctive variety of the dominant language. These 'accents' are usually interpreted simply as arising from the influence of the ethnic language(s), and features indeed may be attributed to substratum varieties or to the mother tongue, but they may be maintained and cultivated (consciously or unconsciously) as linguistic markers of ethnic identity (Giles, 1979)" (Saville-Troike 1989:84).

German foreign workers can call upon a distinctive variety of German that reflects their common background and that can be used to mark ethnic identity in their speech as well as in their writing. Like African Americans in the United States, for instance, foreign workers are marked socially by the language they use. As we saw in Chapter 3, Foreign Worker German is usually regarded by lay Germans as one relatively unified, nonstandard variety. Indeed, these "(stereo)typical" features of Foreign Worker German can be utilized by astute writers to make reference to the group as a whole. However, while Foreign Worker German is stable enough to be characterized generally by linguists and even imitated or parodied by the average German,[34] it is nevertheless open to discernible variation from speaker to speaker and, more importantly here, from ethnic group to ethnic group. There are clear patterns of sociolinguistic behavior that mark the interlocutors as belonging to one group or another.

Linguistic features of immigrant literature perform the seemingly paradoxical functions, at one and the same time, of reinforcing and of breaking down ethnic and social barriers in Germany. Individual ethnic differences are explicitly codified and maintained by the use of various linguistic tokens with inherent ethnic value. Where identification with the umbrella group is desired, such differences can be neutralized by the use of generic Foreign Worker German forms. The linguistic tokens we isolate here include phonological features, lexical choices, and less overt markers such as morphological and syntactic variants.

It is not surprising that ethnicity is marked with the greatest frequency on the phonological level, since this is the level of language most commonly open to interference from the L1 and most typically susceptible to substratum effects in successive generations (see Chapter 3). There is a stereotypical pronunciation associated with generic Foreign Worker German that appears in literature, serving to mark off the foreign workers in general from mainstream groups. The italicized phonological features of the following extract from Franco Biondi's remarkable poem "nicht nur gastarbeiterdeutsch" illustrate some generic phonological features of Foreign Worker German:

NICHT NUR GASTARBEITERDEUTSCH

I. die anfänge

m*ai*ne *nix* gut d*oi*tsch.
isch waiss
isch sprech ja
nur gastarb*ai*terd*oi*tsch
und immer problem*a*
d*oi*tsch loite nix *verstee*
was isch sagen
was i*sch* wollen
aber

langsam langsam
geets:

i*sch* je*t*zz meer verstee³⁵

(in Ackermann 1984b:84)

Note here the substitution of [ʃ] for [ç] ("isch"—[ɪʃ]).³⁶ Consonant clusters are frequently reanalyzed in this generic form of Foreign Worker German, as in the reinterpretation of [çt] or [çts] as [ks] ("nix"—[nɪks]), or in the reduction of "jetzt" [jɛtst] to [jɛts]. There is also considerable use of eye dialect³⁷ here: ⟨ai⟩ for ⟨ei⟩ [aɪ] and ⟨oi⟩ for ⟨eu⟩ [ɔɪ] in "gastarb*ai*terd*oi*tsch"; ⟨ai⟩ for ⟨ei⟩ [aɪ] in "m*ai*ne," and ⟨ee⟩ for ⟨eh⟩ [e] in "geets." These nonstandard (eye dialect) spellings are technically closer to the phonetic values of the words in Standard German than the Standard German spellings themselves. Of course, the cumulative effect of this stereotypical, parodic pronunciation is to represent the generic, illiterate, "fresh-off-the-boat" type of immigrant, the Gastarbeiter-Everyman and the universal immigrant experience.

In other works, however, typical differences in pronunciation from one immigrant group to another are represented, such as in the following extracts:³⁸

Greek:
*Guten Tag, Sie **chaben** (cf. haben) mir diese Vorladung geschickt.*
"Good day, you have sent me this summons."

*Also, ich **chabe** (cf. habe) erst Maschinenbau gelernt.*
"Well, first I studied engineering."

*Das ist **chier**. (cf. hier)*
"It's here."

*Ja, das ist **chalt** (cf. halt) ein langes Studium, und ich **chabe**.* (cf. habe)
"Yes, it's a long course of study, you see, and I have ..."

Churensohn. (cf. Hurensohn)
"Bastard."

In these examples we note particularly the substitution of *ch* [x] for *h* [h] in *habe* and *halt* and, perhaps, for [ç] in *hier*, typical of Greek speakers of German.

Arabic:
*Hier mein Buch, schöne **Errsälung**...* (cf. Erzählung)
"Here [is] my book, nice story ..."

This example illustrates the noticeably trilled [r] (*rr*) and the simplification of the affricate [ts] to a simple sibilant, both typical of Arabic speakers of German.

Italian:
*Ich nic weiß, ich vorher Italiano, aber **jest** nix Italiano, ich Gastarbeiter.* (cf. jetzt)
"I no know I before Italiano but now no Italiano, I Gastarbeiter."

This example illustrates the reduction of the consonant cluster [tst] to [st], in contrast to [ts] as in the generic pronunciation exemplified above.

Turkish:
*Kind nix wegnehmen. Yassin brav, nur **schipilen**, Kind muß.* (cf. spielen)
"Child no take away. Yassin good, only play, child must."

*Du müssen nix atmen. Luft **pirivat**.* (cf. privat)
"You must no breathe. Air private (property)."

*Du können auch Regierung holen, wir hier **bileiben**.* (cf. bleiben)
"You can even government fetch, we here stay."

(Schami 1988:10–34)

These examples illustrate typical Turkish German pronunciation, involving the breaking up of initial consonant clusters with an epenthetic vowel. Such linguistically minor differences in pronunciation nevertheless serve as very strong literary symbols of ethnic identity. Note also that the above examples almost all contain instances of generic Foreign Worker German pronunciation as well, thus at one and the same time marking membership in the umbrella group and maintaining ethnic subgroup differences.

In terms of vocabulary, we note in Biondi's "generic" "nicht nur gastarbeiterdeutsch" the use of *nix gut* ("not good") instead of Standard German *schlecht* ("bad"), a circumlocution typical of all immigrants of comparable linguistic ability, as well as the use of reduplication in *langsam langsam* ("slowly slowly") instead of the standard *sehr langsam* ("very slowly"); there is also the use of the archiform *nix* as opposed to Standard German *nicht* ("not"), *nichts* ("nothing"), and *kein* ("no"). These are characteristics that we included in the table of typical features of Foreign Worker German in Chapter 3. Such "generic" usage can be contrasted with the specific use of the term *Italiano* in the Italian example which is ethnically marked for "Italian-ness."

Morphological and syntactic markers are more difficult to assess. Missing copula examples are generic.

maine ___ nix gut doitsch
"mine ___ not good German"
Hier ___ mein Buch
"here ___ my book"

Ich sechs Jahre . . . nein Monate in Deutschland.
"I six years . . . no months in Germany."
Ich allein.
"I alone."
Mein Deutsch nicht gut.
"My German not good."
    (extracted from Melek Baklan, "Mißverständnis,"
    in Özkan and Wörle 1985:108)

On the other hand, there are differences in the treatment of inflection of predicates that may be accidental or intentional markers of ethnic style in Foreign Worker German:

Generic:
isch sprech
"I speak"
doitsch loite nix verstee
"German people no understand"

Turkish:
Du müssen nix atmen.
"You must not breathe."
Ich arbeiten in Fabrik.
"I work in factory."
Er nicht kommen.
"He is not coming."

In these examples the generic form uses verbal stems and omits desinences, while the Turkish form uses infinitives. Though I have not seen the use of infinitives as verbal archiforms discussed for Turkish speakers specifically, Dittmar (1989:44) has recently shown that Polish migrants in particular typically use what is technically the third person singular present tense form as an archetypal, uninflected form in their learner dialect, so that we might indeed be dealing here with a token that the writer is consciously employing to mark "Turkishness." Since many of the immigrant writers, though not necessarily trained linguists,[39] have a very fine ear for linguistic variability, this observation might usefully be followed up. Even here, these tokens can be used as variable developmental phenomena, not as static fixers of identity, but as situational markers. One of the most remarkable things about Biondi's poem "nicht nur gastarbeiterdeutsch" is the way in which the poet reflects the linguistic development of the immigrant across time.

I do not wish to give the impression here that linguistic markers alone are responsible for the construction of identity in the literary works (or, indeed, in real life!). While we concentrate here on individual linguistic tokens for the purposes of exposition, we must bear in mind, of course, that in context it is a sketch picture that a writer wishes to paint in the broadest strokes and that signifiers of ethnicity are not always linguistic; for example, their ethnic identity may be represented by explicit names and titles or thematically. However, there is no question that the linguistic markers of identity play a significant role in these works, reinforcing the opinion of a number of critics such as Weinrich that one must look carefully at the manipulation of language even in these earlier immigrant texts.

Of course, it is not only the immigrants who have pronunciation problems that reinforce the differences between Germans and immigrants. A recurrent scenario in the literature is the difficulty Germans have pronouncing the names of foreign workers:

»Ja, Herr *Adonis* . . . «
»*Mudopulos* . . .« korrigierte der Grieche und fügte erklärend hinzu »Adonis ist mein Vorname«.
»Ja, Herr *Monopolos* . . .«[40]

(Schami 1988:10–11)

Ein Kolonnenschieber stellt mir eine Stempelkarte aus. . . . Er nimmt Anstoß an meinem Namen: »Das ist doch kein Name. Das ist eine Krankheit. Das kann doch kein Mensch schreiben.« Ich muß ihn mehrfach buchstabieren: S-i-g-i-r-l-i-o-g-l-u. Er notiert ihn dennoch falsch als »Sinnlokus« und setzt ihn an die Stelle des Vornamens. Aus meinem zweiten Vornamen Levent wird der Nachname gemacht. »Wie kann man nur so einen Namen haben« beruhigt er sich bis zuletzt nicht, obwohl sein eigener »Symanowski« oder so ähnlich für einen Türken wohl auch seine Schwierigkeiten hätte....[41]

(Wallraff 1985:87)[42]

Wie heißt du? Kerstin? Nein, Nesrin! Nersin, Nesrir, ach Nesrin!![43]
(Özkan 1985:52).

In a different way here, writers use language to construct the identity of their protagonists. This time the difficulty is in the mouths of the mainstream Germans, who either cannot or will not pronounce non-German names correctly.

Ethnonyms

On the whole, then, we see that the boundaries between groups, while dynamic and sometimes fuzzy, are nevertheless clearly and palpably divisible into mainstream German versus generic Gastarbeiter versus the discrete ethnicities within this generic group. This differentiation between the larger group of Gastarbeiter and the smaller ethnic subgroups is also codified in the euphemistic expressions used for immigrants. Immigrants are frequently divided ethnically according to, among other things, stereotypical custom, occupation, culinary habit, or geographical provenance. As with the linguistic tokens just discussed, ethnonyms are sometimes used to collapse all ethnic groups into one supergroup of immigrant workers, while at other times to clearly differentiate subgroups according to perceived individual ethnic characteristics. The following list of commonly encountered ethnonyms is not intended to be exhaustive, but rather generally illustrative of the terms used:

General (all immigrants)
Gastarbeiter	"guest worker"
Fremde(r)	"stranger"
Ausländer	"foreigner"
Kanake	"South Seas islander"
(cf. *Kanaka*	Hawaiian for "man")
Türke	"Turk"

More specific
Türke	"Turk"
Ittaker	"Italian"

Spaghettifresser "Italian"
Polack "Pole"
Russki "Russian"

That all foreigners are prone to being lumped together is a social fact that has not escaped scholarly attention in other fields. In a sociological exploration of xenophobia in Germany, Hoffmann and Even (1984:71) observe that "[d]ie Begriffe 'Ausländer' und 'Türke' haben in der Alltagssprache häufig schon dieselbe Bedeutung angenommen und können beliebig miteinander vertauscht werden."[44] For this reason, I have termed "Türke" both as a generic and as a specific ethnonym. This is a convention that literary figures have also used. As mentioned above, Schami and Biondi have declared that "Jeder Ausländer ist ein Türke" (1988:49). The list of examples here shows that a number of terms apart from "Türke" are synonymous with generic foreigner, but the term "Türke" is more easily singled out because Turks have for some time constituted that largest and most visibly "different" ethnic minority in Germany.[45] The following poem by Zacharieva is a poignant example of the collective melding together of ethnicities and another reminder that this is not only the custom of the Germans, but also of the foreigners themselves:

ICH sitze
in englisch möblierten Zimmern,
trinke Tee,
genieße.
Wir beide wissen,
daß ich eigentlich auf einem Koffer sitze
irgendwo,
und niste mich ein
zwischen Türken und Griechen.
Schließe die Augen
– ein Schwamm,
dürr von Kompromissen,
lauter Mode
und besserem Wissen.
Sauge auf
etwas Wehmut und Heimweh,
bin enttäuscht, daß nur einer
von diesen Türken und Griechen
nach Knoblauch riecht,
und begeistert, will ich ihm
etwas sagen,

doch er zeigt mir
schweigend
sein Portmonnaie.[46]

(Rumjana Zacharieva 1979, in *Fegefeuer*)

Many of the more insulting terms for foreigners—what Greenberg, Kirkland, and Pyszczyski (1988) refer to as "derogatory ethnic labels"—have to do with eating habits, physical characteristics, and/or animal terms:

Stinktier	"smelly animal"
Knoblauchjuden	"garlic Jews'
Knoblauchfresser	"garlic eaters"[47]
Hammelohr	"sheep's ear"
Affenstall	"monkey stable"[48]

While such ethnonyms are occasionally used by the target group itself, often laconically and sometimes even proprietorily, these more insulting terms are more frequently used by some Germans as ethnic slurs on specific groups:

Arab:	*Kameltreiber, Mulitreiber* "camel driver"
	Sandfresser "sand eater"
Turk:	*Kümmeltürke* "caraway Turk" (and other terms used for Arabs)
Italian:	*Mafioso*
	Spaghettis
	Knoblauchatem "garlic breath"
	Itaka, It(t)aker "Italian"
	Eseltreiber "donkey driver"
African:	*Neger*
	Schwarze(r) "black"
	Moor
	Brickett "briquet"
Asian:	*Schlitzauge* "slant-eye"
	Mandelauge "almond eye"[49]

Moreover, stigmatizing ethnonyms have also developed in the home countries for immigrants who have chosen to return home, such as *almançi* (Turkish); *germanos* (Spanish, cf. *anglos*); *germanesi* (Italian) (Hoffmann and Even 1984:154).

The Developmental Nature of Foreign Worker Literature

Most of the observations we have made so far about the use of language in creating identity apply more readily to considerations of earlier immigrant works than more recent ones. The reason for this is that, just as the language of immigrants is not a static phenomenon, so the literature of immigrants is also dynamic and moves on to deal with new themes and develop new linguistic and literary forms.

There is a discernible development in immigrant German literature that mirrors the general pattern of linguistic development in quite a striking fashion. Foreign worker literature has progressed from its beginnings as a rather restricted form of communication, limited in scope, themes, and form, to its present status as a variety of literature that is knocking on the door of mainstream German literature and that deserves to be measured by current standard criteria, rather than be treated as a separate (non-German, exotic, or inferior) genre.

This progression is, conceptually speaking, remarkably similar to the linguistic development. We recall from Chapter 3 that Foreign Worker German displays a natural development that is similar to all other contact varieties of language. It develops out of two contact languages into an extremely reduced or basilectal form of communication that is restricted in scope to situations of communicative necessity. Once it has stabilized and becomes a principal means of communication for a group of speakers, it expands in function and form, developing structures that are unique and not present in either of the contact languages. Finally, after gaining acceptance or tolerance by the prestige society, it typically develops in the direction of the standard, lexifier, or superstrate language, often supplanting creole features with standard ones, but still retaining a substratum effect from its contact origins. This process of linguistic development is illustrated in Figure 9 in the preceding chapter.

As illustrated in Figure 11, foreign worker literature appears to undergo a parallel development, albeit with some significant differences. A crude, functionally reduced, and formally unstable kind of pre-literature develops out of contact between the home and the host culture, which is the product of an urgent need to communicate. Once conditions stabilize, the literature expands to meet the changing needs of the writers, and it develops its own particular characteristics that are different from both the literature of the home country (Lit1), and from mainstream German literature (Lit2). As it gains acceptance, it begins to shift in terms of form and models in the direction of mainstream German literature, while still retaining a substratum effect from its contact background.[50]

Language, Literature, and Identity 125

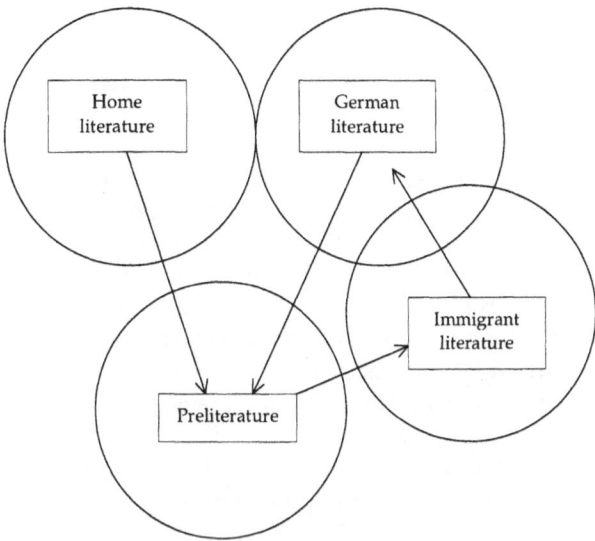

Figure 11. Development of Immigrant Literature

This progression is reflected in three major observable stages of immigrant literature, which are inextricably linked to the struggle for identity, and which we can refer to as the loss phase, the reconstruction phase, and the consolidation phase.

The first phase is marked by existential issues. It is restricted to themes such as the loss of home, family, rights, language, voice, and identity, and its major function is as a "Klammer- und Klagephase" (Raddatz 1994:45), in which many, if not most, of the literary productions are crude and ignore considerations of form. Communication in this phase is self-centered. While there is often a direct appeal to an imaginary other, there is no real dialogue; the author is in an imposed monologic relationship, reflecting the linguistic and social reality of his or her environment, and is struggling to find a place and a voice in the new society. Raitz (1989:292–93) provides a description of Gastarbeiterliteratur that is a succinct illustration of this phase, which I have distilled into the following major points:

1. The vast majority of this literature consists of lyrical texts and short prose.
2. Structures are strikingly epic, often consisting of one, two, or three sentences whose words are in "poetic" form, either in rhyming couplets or, in the majority of cases, unrhymed.

3. The greater proportion of the narratives is oriented toward everyday narration: simple orders of events dominate without any great narrative-technical complications. Only occasionally are there flashbacks, interwoven dreams, and dialogues.
4. The syntax is simple and paratactic.
5. The "message" is very often in the narrator's commentary or is directly stated by one of the protagonists. Sometimes it is even accentuated visually, as if the authors are not sure of the power of this form of expression that is so new to them.
6. There is a dominant antithetical form, reflecting "life in two worlds," which sometimes leads to oversimplified black-and-white contrasts.
7. If there is any orientation toward literary models and forms, it is toward amorphous forms in the folk-literature of the home country, poems learned in primary school, dialect poems, carnival satire, jokes, and popular songs.

Raitz also imputes to this early literature a "zunächst eher sedative und autotherapeutische Funktion" ("primarily sedative and autotherapeutic function"), coupled with the search for and expression of individual and group identity as a guest worker and member of a minority (293).

There are numerous examples of this phase in both poetry and prose (and especially in the early collections mentioned above, produced by organizations such as PoLiKunst). As an illustration we might cite the following poem by Pasquale Marino, which elsewhere (Fennell 1994) I have singled out for the remarkable way in which it mirrors the internal "pecking order" amongst immigrants on the one hand, and characterizes the successive stages of acquisition of German syntax on the other:

VERSTEHEN

Ich Türke. Nix verstehen!
Ich Grieche. Deutsch nix verstehen!
Ich Jugoslawe. Nicht Deutsch verstehen!
Ich bin Spanier. Ich nicht verstehe Deutsch!
Ich bin Italiener. Ich verstehe nicht gut Deutsch!
Ich bin Deutscher. Ich verstehe euch alle nicht![51]

(in Taufiq 1983)

Perhaps an even better example is the following attempt at a poem by Sadi Üçüncü, with its simplistic structure and vocabulary and its heavy-handed message:

Ich bin der Ausländer
der letzte Dreck

auf der Erde
schäme mich
auf der Straße,
in der Kneipe,
in der Diskothek
mit meinem schwarzen Haar,
schwarzen Augen,
schwarzen Schnurrbart
und
dunkler Haut
von Natur aus stigmatisiert

Ich bin der Ausländer
der letzte Dreck
auf der Erde

Niemand spricht mit mir,
niemand besucht mich
Ich, Ausländer,
nichts verstehen, nichts sprechen
Ich bin der Ausländer
der letzte Dreck
auf der Erde[52]

(1984:vii)

The second phase involves the reconstruction of identity, in which the writer strives to adapt to the new culture and the new environment, while tenaciously resisting giving up the old. The content and form of this phase are generally variable, and still in the main quite different from both the literature of the home country and mainstream German literature. A good example of this might be the following extract from Adel Karasholi's poem "Daheim in der Fremde" ("At Home Abroad"), written originally between 1977 and 1984:

Meine zwei Länder und ich
Wir sind vermählt
Bis daß der Tod uns scheidet
Und jetzt bin ich hier
Unter euch
Mit euch
Und ich lasse nicht ab von mir
Und von euch[53]

(1992:69)

The third phase marks the consolidation of the new identity. Here, the writers directly engage the canon, question and critique received criticism and enter into a true dialogue with the society and the culture. Though literary productions still display a substratum effect or trace of their hybrid background, immigrant literature at this phase is a variation within German literature, not some exotic outsider activity. During this phase writers assert their identity *as writers*, concern themselves with form and their relationship with German literature, and demand participation in German literary life, and recognition and respect from all quarters.

While these parallels between the development of the language and the literature have not to my knowledge been discussed explicitly before, they can hardly be considered surprising. After all, the development of literature is essentially dependent on language, and both are in turn dependent upon cultural and psychosocial development. Just as speakers begin with the L1 alone and develop a means of communication under the total dominance of the L2, so writers begin from Lit1 and develop a means to communicate under the dominance of Lit2. And some, who were not active in Lit1, have to make the huge jump from the L1 alone to the L2/Lit2. In both instances, the host society dictates the form of emergent communication, and its norms are those by which the product is judged, often in ignorance, or even in explicit denial of, the legitimacy of variants that emerge under the influence of the speaker's or writer's individual background. Thus, speakers with a desire to be integrated inevitably shift in the direction of the standard, and writers similarly shift their gaze toward the national literary standard. Given the right circumstances, this can lead to acceptance and to a shift in the conception of the linguistic or literary mainstream.

The first two stages of this progression can be detected in the following passage from Özkan und Wörle:

> Als vor einigen Jahren ausländische Frauen und Männer zu schreiben begannen, ging es wohl zunächst darum, Einsamkeit und Isolation zu überwinden und negative Erfahrungen zu bewältigen. Mit dem Schritt an die Öffentlichkeit kam die Erkenntnis, daß man/frau nicht alleine war. Es entstand Solidarität unter den Betroffenen, und der Zugang zum deutschen Leser, der sich ebenso betroffen fühlen mußte, wurde dadurch erleichtert, daß man die deutsche Sprache als Vehikel für die Auseinandersetzung mit der deutschen Realität wählte. Wenn Ausländer/innen heute deutsch schreiben, so wollen sie nicht nur Verständnis für Fremdartigkeit wecken und dadurch den Umgang erleichtern, sondern sie wollen

auch Einfluß nehmen auf die deutsche Wirklichkeit, zu deren Bestandteil sie geworden sind. Sie wollen Widerstand leisten gegen Gesetze und Verordnungen, die die Integration erschweren und die Isolation befördern. Sie wollen aktiv am gesellschaftlichen, politischen und kulturellen Leben teilnehmen, und sie wollen die Entscheidung, zu bleiben, oder zu gehen, freiwillig treffen, ohne massivem rechtlichem und gesellschaftlichem Druck ausgesetzt zu werden.[54]

(1985:8)

However, in the last seven or eight years, immigrant writers' demands have changed: they want all of the things that Özkan und Wörle mention, but they also want urgently to be recognized as writers and intellectuals. It is an inevitable consequence of being able to write literature that sells and develops a following that immigrant authors now wish for their literature to be taken seriously and regarded as *literature*. They also want to be considered no longer exotic, or non-German, to break out of the mold of Gastarbeiterliteratur, and to be accepted into the mainstream as legitimate writers of *German* literature. That this is the issue is attested by a number of recent articles and comments by some of the most successful writers themselves. These pronouncements herald the third phase of immigrant literature, in which immigrant writers want to assert their literary identity, to make their contribution to German literature and cultural life, and to enter into a dialogue with mainstream authors and critics. For Yüksel Pazarkaya, this is clearly a point of frustration:

Wir leben am Rande auch der literarischen Gesellschaft dieses Landes. Keinem von uns ist zum Beispiel die Gelegenheit gegeben, als Gastdozent an der Frankfurter Universität über seine Ästhetik zu lesen. Ich kann mir durchaus vorstellen, daß Biondi oder ich in der Lage wären, versuchsweise die ästhetischen Ansätze unserer Literatur, unserer Dichtung universitär darzulegen und das dann im Anschluß zu publizieren, worüber dann auch diskutiert werden kann. . . . Und das wird nicht gewürdigt, von keiner Institution, von keinem Verlag, von keinem deutschen Kollegen, von niemandem.[55]

(cited in Raddatz 1994:46)

Clearly the last sentence is an exaggeration, given the fact that the cry for recognition is not heard only from within the immigrant writers' community. As we pointed out above, critics such as Weinrich and

Ackermann have long been interested in such works as literature. In his recent article in *Die Zeit*, critic Fritz J. Raddatz assesses the work of a number of immigrant writers, including José F. A. Oliver, Gino Chiellino, Zafir Senocak, and Franco Biondi. While he recognizes the long road immigrant literature has traveled to reach its current position, he is extremely sensitive to its particular linguistic and cultural genius and to the special kind of linguistic precision it entails:

> Sie bringen nicht nur Fremd-Worte ein (wie Zehra Çıraks "Zufallsfeige" für des Vaters Ohrfeige einen schönen fremden Geschmack assoziiert), und sie schmuggeln auch nicht lediglich ungewohnte Fracht wie Zikaden oder Honigmelonen; das zu benoten scheint mir gar am Rande einer schiefmäuligen Kopftuch-Solidarität. Gemeint ist vielmehr eine Wortgenauigkeit, eine Härte, mit der Silben, Töne, Klänge auf den Prüfstand gelegt, neu abgehorcht und neu erarbeitet (bearbeitet?) werden.[56]

(1994:46).

The "disadvantage" of being a nonnative speaker can become a major asset of a wordsmith, and new coinages and ways of speaking result, which enrich German language and culture as a whole. What has been lacking from immigrant literature until this point has been the quality and sophistication of form that allow it to be compared with established German prose and poetry. Raddatz is one of the critics to liken at least the later work of foreign writers to that of established German literary figures. In particular, he praises the formal complexity and perfection of the poetry of José F. A. Oliver (a second-generation Spanish immigrant, actually born in Germany). An example of this is Oliver's poem "im gerippe eines tages" ("in the skeleton of a day"):

> ich schenke euch ein wörterbuch/ euch und mir/ ein uns kein dach
> und diesem land/ ein haus/ gemach
> aus nichts und wort
> aus wort um wort
> aus und –
> aus sprachenhäuten/ hoy ein heute
> ist grün ist weiß ist schnee ein fenster
> weit so weit
>
> ich schenke euch mein wörterbuch
> nicht meiner fremde – ojo!
> de*n* einsamkeiten/ meiner Haut und
> deutschland, meinland – dir

auch und immer undland und/ und
deutsch land außer sicht/ land menschvergessen
dies land ist/...

... ein tod wie Auschwitz immernoch

kein neotod kein neomord/ kein neu und neo kein/ und Kain:
mord und tod bleibt gleich/ sagt

ein tod wie Auschwitz immernoch?[57]

(in Raddatz 1994:46)

To Oliver's work, I believe we can add the troubled, haunting poetry of the Syrian Adel Karasholi, who in his latest work extends the theme of tortured exile far beyond a simple clash of two cultures into an internalized, intensely personal quest for self:

FREMDER TOD

Entwurzelt
Und verwachsen mit fremdem Tod
Werfe ich mich ab
Nacht
Für Nacht
Von mir

Offenes Grab
Meine dünne Haut
Kälte böse Blicke
Dringt ungehindert
Ein und aus

Rückwärtsgewandt
Breche ich auf
In den kommenden Tag[58]

Not just poets, but prose writers, too, have reached a standard comparable to mainstream German literary standards. Franco Biondi's new novel *Die Unversöhnlichen—Im Labyrinth der Herkunft* ("The Irreconcilable—In Provenance's Labyrinth") is hailed as a first-rate work, and its complex interwoven plot of real and unreal characters (including Biondi himself) is described by Raddatz as "eine essayistische Lektion über Schreiben und Identität allemal" ("certainly a lesson on writing and identity in essay form") (1994:46). Though he still has questions about Biondi's sometimes faulty German and his "precious" coinages,

Raddatz acclaims Biondi as "nicht nur ein glänzender, sprachmächtiger und bildstarker Erzähler, sondern auch ein raffiniert mit den Mitteln moderner Prosa jonglierender Romancier."[59]

Another significant indicator of the coming of age of immigrant literature is the fact that it is being translated into English and published abroad. Here we might mention the great success of Rafik Schami's collection *Eine Hand voller Sterne*, published in English translation as *A Handful of Stars* by Gollancz Press of London in 1990 and republished in paperback by Penguin the following year. Akif Pirinçci (the second-generation author who also keeps his distance from his immigrant past, yet who writes about a cat detective as an outsider who is far more astute than the cats on the inside) has had three works translated into English (published by Fourth Estate in London), including the two cat detective novels, *Felidae* (1993) and *Felidae on the Road* (1994). Furthermore, *Felidae* itself has been released in a cartoon version starring, amongst others, Rainer-Maria Brandauer, and has developed something of a cult following amongst young Germans. Libuse Monikova's recent successful novel has also been published in English as *The Façade* by Chatto and Windus of London (1992), though again, Monikova might need to be considered separately in that she has never been a Gastarbeiter. As a proponent of *immigrant* literature, however, she is worth citing in this context.

Literature as Capital: National and Intellectual Forces in the Negotiation of Identity

The third and current phase of development is by no means complete, however, and immigrant writers are still fighting for inclusion in the field of German literature. There have been calls to "reconceptualize our understanding of an identifiably German core of contemporary literature" (Adelson 1990:382) to include immigrant literature under a broadened concept of what it means to be German, and "sich zu lösen von der Gastarbeiterexotik" ("to free oneself from the Gastarbeiter exotic") (Raddatz 1994:45). All of this is most reminiscent of the "canon wars" in the United States and other English-speaking countries, which have also been the subject of Bourdieu's attention. The question remains, why is it so difficult for Germans, or should we say for German *scholars*, to accept immigrant literature as part of German literature? To answer this question and by way of conclusion, we need to consider the disparate forces that contribute to the construction of the identity of German immigrants.

Let us recall the passage from Biondi, in which he claims that "someone" invented the term "Gastarbeiter," someone who did not know immigrants, but who was aware of the profit to be made from this word and who made profit from it. We have seen that Chiellino also lamented that the unfortunate linking of Gastarbeiterdeutsch and *Betroffenheit* had the effect of relegating immigrant literature to being the object of study by sociologists and linguists, rather than by literary critics. These, I feel, are telling points of view that give us important insights into the struggle for identity.

That immigrants have reacted skeptically to linguists' and sociologists' activities is hardly surprising. By using terms such as "Pidgindeutsch" and "Gastarbeiterdeutsch" that incorporate stigmatized elements, and by comparing immigrant linguistic performance with Standard German, they have been effectively, if unwittingly, acting as linguistic gatekeepers and as agents of that standard, reinforcing the status quo, representing the establishment, and determining the fate of immigrant writers.

It might therefore seem incongruous that immigrant writers themselves at first espoused the notions "Gastarbeiter" and "Gastarbeiterdeutsch," using them as a rallying cry in both literary works and commentaries. Was this simply shortsightedness on their part, or was something more at stake here? A partial answer would seem to lie in the immigrant writers' attitudes toward language and identity, given their position as the intellectual elite of the immigrant minorities. Research in sociology has produced some rather remarkable findings on the role of language as a symbol of group identity in multilingual societies. Contrary to the expectations of experts, multilingual groups in South American communities (for example, the Yucatec Mayans) did not regard their home language as essential to their ethnic identity and declared it would be more of a problem for them if they were to lose Spanish. Furthermore, they expressed a preference for a monolingual, Spanish school system over a Mayan-language school system. These linguistic attitudes prevailed despite the fact that on other grounds they distinguished very strictly between ethnic groups in their region (Kummer 1990:265). This is a clear indication that for ordinary people there is no necessary link between language and ethnic identity, so that it is not so exceptional for immigrant writers to claim group allegiance on the one hand, but finally to dissociate themselves from Gastarbeiterdeutsch on the other.

Kummer proposes that it is the elite who play a decisive role in promoting language as a marker of ethnic identity. He provides the following summary of the work of the Austrian marxist philosopher Otto

Bauer (1907), which illuminates the essential connection between the modernization of traditional agrarian societies and the development of an ethnically conscious intelligentsia in a dependent minority leaning toward modernization:

1. The use of language as a marker of cultural identity presupposes the development of an ethnic intelligentsia in a social conflict, in which a group, which can be separated off by a more or less common language, finds itself in an oppressed situation, such as the occupation of their territory by another group, as a minority within another group's territory, or as a colonized group, etc.
2. For the oppressed group the social conflict is typically linked with a change in the socioeconomic structure, such as the transition from agrarian to capitalist methods of production, rapid industrialization, or modernization.
3. The ethnic intelligentsia constitutes or supports the leadership of the oppressed minority in the social conflict and uses cultural identity as a weapon in this struggle as well as a means to secure its own power within its own group.
4. Language as a marker of cultural identity is always used in conjunction with other possible cultural markers, such as religion, oral or written literary tradition, etc. This connection stresses the values of the premodern society, which is in the process of social change, although the definition of the cultural identity is used as a weapon to gain better opportunities in the modernizing society.

(Kummer 1990:267)

This model of ethnogenesis assumes, according to Kummer, that the choice of language as a central symbol of cultural identity arises as a defensive means of constructing an identity for use by an ethnic intelligentsia in confrontation with a dominating or colonizing society. This, he argues, explains the pragmatic indifference of the majority, which does not share the aspirations of power that the intelligentsia has and which more readily assimilates to the cultural models of the dominant culture (1990:267).

This theory has some application to the immigrant German question. There is no doubt that, notwithstanding Biondi's criticisms of sociologists and linguists, the immigrant writers in Germany at first also recognized the symbolic, cultural, and economic capital to be made from exploiting a multicultural Gastarbeiter concept and using Gastarbeiterdeutsch as a central emblem. If nothing else, it aided in consciousness-raising and opened the doors of the publishing houses. What backfired, however, was that the use of Gastarbeiterdeutsch, along with labels like *Betroffenheit*, had an extremely constraining effect on the writers themselves. As Raitz (1989:293) puts it, "Das Insistieren auf dem 'Gastarbeiterdeutsch' als Literatursprache ist aber ambivalent, da dies sowohl eine mangelhafte Beherrschung des Deutschen als auch einen kunstfertigen produktiven Umgang mit diesen 'Mängeln' bedeuten kann."[60] Moreover, as Raitz (1994) and a number of other critics (for example, Raddatz and Ackermann) have pointed out, the overall result was a fixed set of expectations about immigrant literature, making it increasingly difficult for immigrant writers to get any work accepted that was not in the Gastarbeiter mold.

Here again we are witnessing that classic rift between the labels that have stuck—the classification, in Bourdieu's terms—and the social structure and social attitudes, which have clearly moved on: "a gap between objective social space and members' representations of that space, a site for symbolic struggles that transform the real by renaming it" (Collins 1993:127). It is for this reason primarily, I believe, that immigrant writers have retracted so precipitously and so absolutely from both the Gastarbeiter concept and Gastarbeiterdeutsch and are now pressing in earnest for an identity as variant ethnicities within the German mainstream. Only in this way, they feel, can they retain their position within the immigrant group as an intellectual elite and receive the recognition thus far denied them by those cultural gatekeepers, the literary critics. What is interesting to note is that, at this stage of development, immigrant writers have nowhere to go *but* toward the German mainstream. They already have a long tradition of creative contributions in Germany, and they have developed so far from their "original" identity as Turk, Italian, Lebanese, etc., that this identity can no longer be a home for them to go to. What is important, as Bourdieu points out in his work *Ce que parler veut dire* (1977), is that the power of discourse is tied to the power of groups; the ability to mobilize a group—to invest a group with identity and will to act—is an essential source of the "power of words." Thus we cannot be surprised that the crucial site of the classification struggle for identity *within* the German framework is being waged by the intellectual immigrant elite against the indigenous academic critics, who are the guardians of the status quo. It will be interesting to follow this argument in the future.

We have talked up to this point about how immigrants have been subjected to the loss of identity and the process of renegotiating it. Perhaps our final words should be reserved for a discussion of the fact that in Germany there is also a larger identity puzzle into which the immigrants must find a way to fit. The Germans themselves have been trapped in an identity crisis throughout their recent history (as any history book or collection of papers on modern literature will attest). Barbour and Stephenson explain that "the Federal Republic is a young state whose physical limits and constitutional status were determined by foreign powers and whose population has had to struggle to come to terms not only with its past but also with the problem of finding a new identity for itself" (1990:192). Since World War II, West Germany has striven to develop the image of a peaceable, democratic, and tolerant country with an exemplary work ethic and progressive technological outlook. Striking occurrences such as the massive influx of immigrants and the reunification with the German Democratic Republic and the enormous adjustments this entailed, coupled with deeper but less obvious developments, such as the decline in birthrate amongst native Germans (see chapter 1), have strained this tolerance, leading native Germans themselves to feel threatened and fearful of losing their identity. The terms, both official and unofficial, used for foreigners and to describe the immigrant-labor process ("Gastarbeiter," "Rotation," "Nicht-Einwanderungsland," "Anwerbeland," etc.) indirectly serve to maintain a separate German identity by reinforcing difference.

In the buildup to recent changes in immigration laws, German newspaper articles frequently featured articles about the link between definitions of nationality and Germany's Nazi past. A popular German opinion is that citizenship in a United Europe would put other citizenships in the background and help to lay the Nazi ghost to rest and contribute to *Vergangenheitsbewältigung* ("coming to terms with the past"). But German lawmakers still hold on to a concept of *ius sanguinis*, and not the *ius solis* definition of nationality common in most of the rest of Europe (see Chapter 1). In so doing, they reinforce the exclusiveness of being German.

The antiforeigner activities in places such as Hoyerswerda, Mölln, and Solingen are severe examples of the effects of insecurity. In a much subtler but nevertheless powerful way, Germans exert their authority through language by insisting on Standard German or on other indigenous German varieties and by gathering all the many varieties of immigrant language together under the rubric "Gastarbeiterdeutsch." Similarly, ethnic separation is maintained and German superiority enforced by lumping all immigrant literary contributions under the heading of "Gastarbeiterliteratur."

Raddatz (1994:45) asks the question why there is no German Salman Rushdie or Kazuo Ishiguro; why the English and French have a long tradition of colonial literature, but Germany does not. I think the answer is clear. Unlike Britain and France, Germany has no history of colonialism; its *Platz an der Sonne* came late and was not of any real significance.[61] As a result, Germany has had only a very short history of linguistic colonialism, unlike, for example, Britain and France. For this reason, I think that Germany is not yet ready to accept colonial or postcolonial models of language and literature. In a way, what we are dealing with in Germany today is a kind of belated, internal, economic colonialism, and, for this reason, issues of identity are still being negotiated—by immigrants and Germans alike.

Notes

Introduction

1. I am grateful to an anonymous reviewer for introducing me to the term "permigrants." While this is not a viable term for use in this study (largely, I confess, for aesthetic reasons), it does seem to capture the exquisite contradiction in the status of long-term foreign worker residents of the Federal Republic. However, I recognize that my own perception is colored by my status as a nonnative academic.

Chapter 1

1. While we use the terms "Pole" and "Polish" here, we must bear in mind that there was no "Poland" as such between 1875 and 1918.
2. Term used by the chairman of the German Arbeitgeberverband ("Employers' Union"), in *Der Arbeitgeber*, 6 (1966):138. Cited in Hamm (1988:25).
3. "Germany is not an immigration country. Our country's capacity to take in refugees must not be overtaxed. Whoever does this is promoting antiforeigner sentiment."
4. These colonies were in various parts of Eastern Europe, including within Prussia itself, within the Habsburg Empire, in Transylvania (the so-called Transylvanian Sachsen), Banat (the Banater Schwaben), Russia, the Volga Colonies, and on the Black Sea.
5. "The political dispute and the headlines in the media are almost interchangeable: you need only replace the word 'Turks' with 'asylum seekers.' In both cases the 'fully laden ship Federal Republic Germany' threatened to capsize, on account of the apparently too high numbers of—then—Turks and—now—refugees and asylum seekers."
6. "The parallels between the Turks then and the asylum seekers today make it clear that little has been learned from the immigration debate. At the beginning of the 1980s, about a million Turks were living in Germany, and their number had ostensibly to be reduced. Today there are almost twice as many, but by now it clearly does not matter any more. Hardly anyone still remembers this context or quotes from responsible politicians such as 'So long as I have a say in Hessen, not another Turk will come into this state.' The same applies to the statement of another politician, who said, 'My goal is the solution of the foreigner problem which basically concerns Turkish families.'"
7. "Turks want to fit in as Turkish members of German society; Germans expect them to shed their Turkish identity."
8. "A German is not someone who is born in Germany—no, a German is someone who is descended from Germans."

9. Though there was a sharp decline in the German economy in late 1995 and early 1996, this has not (yet) altered the projected need for foreign labor in the long term.

Chapter 2

1. Bundesministerium 1989 1:9.
2. *Berlin DIW Wochenbericht*, 11 August 1988:397–408.
3. By comparison, foreigners make up about 8 percent of the population in France, 9 percent in Belgium, 14 percent in Switzerland and 23 percent in Luxembourg (Bundesministerium 1989 1:9).
4. "Guests turned into permanent guests and then immigrants."
5. "They were subjected in puberty to the culture shock associated with immigration, they had an education that was inadequate for our society, they had not learned a profession and did not speak a word of German."
6. See Pommerin (1984) and other articles in the same journal for examples of intercultural language instruction, and *Deutsch als Fremdsprache* for numerous articles on language instruction.
7. Safter Çinar, of the Science and Education Union (Gewerkschaft Wissenschaft und Erziehung) in Berlin, has suggested to me (personal communication) that the actual figures were even higher than the official ones.
8. "Deutschland, das ist wie ein kurierter Alkoholiker. Wehe, wenn er wieder an die Flasche kommt" (American Holocaust historian Raul Hilberg, cited in Bade 1994:199).

Chapter 3

1. While this list is adapted from Bodemann and Ostow (1975:134–45) and all special emphasis is mine, I have reproduced the examples in standard orthography.
2. See Mühlhäusler (1984) for a comprehensive discussion of the sources of reduced forms of German.
3. See Kurz (forthcoming) for a reinterpretation of the categories of restrictive and elaborative simplification.
4. However, other examples from Blackshire-Belay's informants demonstrate that they had a number of verb forms at their disposal and did not rely exclusively on the infinitive (1991:204).
5. See Fox (1990:183–84) for a discussion of the preference for the term "nonpast" over "present."
6. Probably influenced by the parallel construction in Standard German, which occurs in the form of a question, but in fact functions as an indirect command.
7. See Dulay, Burt, and Krashen (1982) and Selinker (1992) for general discussions of second-language acquisition, and Clahsen, Meisel, and Pienemann

Notes to Pages 58–65   141

(1983) for a comparative discussion of the acquisition of German as a first or second language.

8. By "adjuncts," Dittmar is referring here to relative pronouns, embedded *wh*-words, and complementizers.

9. This is, of course a cross-sectional, not a longitudinal, study; as such, any developmental sequence implicit in its findings takes place in apparent time only.

10. For the sake of the nonspecialist reader, I have attempted to render these examples in "phonetically sensitive" regular spelling, adapting the original examples, which are in phonetic transcription.

11. Indeed, in a more recent study, Kurz (forthcoming) finds that immigrants who have had prior experience with non-German second-language acquisition before arrival in Germany are more successful at acquiring German.

12. To say nothing of the psycholinguistic barriers to learners attempting to acquire a second language after puberty, that is, according to the "critical age" hypothesis.

13. "It should also be borne in mind here that the form chosen by the foreign workers corresponds neither to Swabian nor to colloquial German."

14. "Der Begriff 'Pidgin-Deutsch' wird im Rahmen dieses Beitrages nicht im strengen Sinne des Terminus 'Pidgin' verwendet, der für spezifische Sprachkontaktsituationen in Kolonialländern entwickelt worden ist.... Bei der Verwendung des Begriffs 'Pidgin-Deutsch' lassen wir uns von zwei allgemeinen Gesichtspunkten leiten.

Erstens bezeichnet der Begriff ebensowenig wie der Terminus 'die deutsche Sprache' eine in sich *homogene* Sprache. Vielmehr faßt er bestimmte Varietäten des Deutschen zusammen, die spezifische linguistische und soziale Merkmale gemeinsam haben und in vorläufiger Abgrenzung zu anderen Sprachformen mit dem Begriff 'Pidgin-Deutsch' belegt werden können.

Zweitens bezieht sich der Begriff auf jene Varietät des Deutschen, die Arbeitsimmigranten unter ähnlichen sozialen Bedingungen erlernen. Wir unterscheiden somit Lernkontexte, in denen eine Zweitsprache unter sehr unterschiedlichen *individuellen* Umständen erlernt wird, von solchen Kontexten, in denen die überwiegende Anzahl einer Gruppe von Zweitsprachenlernern eine fremde Sprache unter gleichen oder ähnlichen *sozialen* Bedingungen erwirbt. Im Sinne dieses Unterschiedes untersuchen wir nicht syntaktische Eigenschaften der Varietäten von Individuen, sondern von Gruppen.

Unter 'Pidgin-Deutsch' verstehen wir das mehr oder weniger stark vereinfachte Deutsch ausländischer Arbeiter, das sie in der Regel nur aufgrund der Notwendigkeiten und des Alltags in der BRD in sozial begrenzten Kontakten mit Deutschen und Ausländern anderer Nationalitäten erwerben. Im wesentlichen trifft der Terminus auf das rudimentäre Deutsch jener ausländischer Arbeiter zu, die sich aufgrund des Kooperationszwanges am Arbeitsplatz zum Zwecke der Verständigung einer Varietät des Deutschen bedienen müssen, in ihrer Freizeit jedoch wenig oder kein Deutsch sprechen—es sei denn, um Probleme alltäglicher Bedürfnisse wie etwa Einkaufen, Arztbesuche etc. zu regeln. Die zur Verrichtung der Arbeit meist nur in geringem Maße erforderlichen Deutschkenntnisse sind in routinierten Interaktionen am Arbeitsplatz erlernt. Diese arbeitsbedingten, meist oberflächlichen Kommunikationskontakte führen in der Regel zu einem sozial eingespielten Gebrauch einer vereinfachten Varietät des Deutschen, die auf einem bestimmten Niveau der Sprachbeherrschung 'eingefroren' ist."

15. For a comprehensive discussion of foreigner talk, see Ferguson (1971: 143) and Holm (1988:33), as well as the papers by Meisel (1975a, 1975b) and Hinnenkamp (1990).

16. It might be considered an exaggeration to say that foreign spouses live for years in total isolation. This is a matter of debate, however. It is clearly the case that foreign women often live in isolation from the rest of society, as the following official quotation from the Bundesministerium für Frauen und Jugend attests:

> Ausländische Frauen leben oft sehr isoliert. Die Kontakte außerhalb der Familie werden meist von den Männern wahrgenommen; die Kinder, die in deutsche Schulen gehen, beherrschen die deutsche Sprache besser als ihre Mütter. So entstehen Unsicherheit und Konflikte. . . . Die nicht erwerbstätigen Frauen leiden oft darunter, daß sie einen großen Teil des Tages in der Wohnung verbringen müssen. Anders als im Heimatland, wo sich das Leben meist außerhalb des Hauses abspielt, müssen sie hier alles auf engem Raum in der Wohnung erledigen.
> (*Frauen in der Bundesrepublik Deutschland*, official publication of the Bundesministerium für Frauen und Jugend, 1992:107)

17. I choose, à la Selinker (1972, 1992), to apply the term "interlanguage" to the intermediate systems of L2 learners (though I still acknowledge the differences between L1 and L2 learning).

18. While school is compulsory in Germany, it is well known that there is a significant number of foreign children who "fall through the cracks," often because their parents choose not to send them to school.

19. For a discussion of factors affecting the acquisition of German by second-generation Serbs and Croats, see Stölting (1973). Stölting mentions in particular the significance of age on immigration of the second generation, a factor which Biehle was unable to consider in his study.

20. Note that I am using the term "xenolect" in this specific way, not as it is used by Roche (1989). Roche applies it to the way in which nonnative speakers alter their language when accommodating nonnative speakers, a phenomenon which I term "foreigner talk," in keeping with researchers such as Ferguson (1971), Holm (1988), and Romaine (1988).

21. This is reminiscent of the characterization of African American Vernacular English as a creoloid variety, which contains such morphological reductions as the lack of plurals after numbers, e.g., *two book*, but which does not (any longer?) show any radical restructuring of Standard American English.

22. Though a number of native German speakers assure me that such varieties exist.

23. This seems to me to be close to the definition of xenolect that I have just given: it is "foreignized," but not radically restructured.

24. Presumably, when she equates lexical with analytic expressions, Kotsinas is referring to such features as using phrasal verbs and adverbs to denote time reference, as opposed to using morphological markers of tense.

25. For "opaque," read "irregular."

26. However, there has been a considerable amount of work on identity marking, group consciousness, etc., in the language of bilingual, second-generation immigrant youth—see Auer (1984), di Luzio (1984), and discussion in Gal (1987). Robin M. Queen (University of Texas at Austin) is apparently working on the intonation of German-dominant ethnic Turkish children.

27. Acrolect differs from the standard in that it usually retains a trace of the substrate language.

28. "Phase 1: 'Gastarbeiterdeutsch" als zu entdeckender Code: Was ist anders, was fehlt gegenüber die Zielsprache? (z.B. Clyne 1968, Orlovic-Schwarzwald 1978)

"Phase 2: 'Gastarbeiterdeutsch' als soziolinguistisches Phänomen: Welche außersprachlichen Faktoren bedingen den ungesteuerten Spracherwerb? (z.B. HDP 1975ff.)

"Phase 3: 'Gastarbeiterdeutsch' als interaktionales Problem und Produkt: Wie bedingen Kommunikationsprozesse zwischen Mutter- und Nichtmuttersprachlern den Erwerbs- und Verständigungsprozeß? (z.B. Kutsch/Desgranges 1985)."

29. Elwira Grossman has kindly given me the following popular Polish saying to illustrate this use of the instrumental: *Wyrzuc go drzwiami, to oknem wlezie* ("if you throw him out of the door, he'll come back through the window"—used to describe a persistent, intrusive, obtrusive person.

30. I do not think it makes a difference here that Antek had received some formal language training. I doubt very much whether he had been taught the strategy of extension of meaning in his Goethe Institute course.

31. For a discussion of other communication strategies in Foreign Worker German, see, for example, Dittmar (1984).

32. Arguably, such subfields as African American linguistics, feminist linguistics, scientific German, and legal German do indeed exist, but the broader point of Hinnenkamp's argument still holds.

33. While this can be disputed, the negative reaction of foreign writers to the concept of "Gastarbeiterdeutsch," which we shall discuss in the next chapter, suggests that they at least share Hinnenkamp's view.

34. "In no way can Gastarbeiter-status be regarded as the precondition for that learner language, which has been reflected in the description and analysis of 'Gastarbeiterdeutsch.' Subsuming whole catalogs of linguistic deficits under one panethnic and social category and linking a 'deficit-laden' variety of German with a social and panethnic category could only serve to strengthen the *special status* of this category. For, of all the *possible* distin-

guishing criteria vis-à-vis 'Germans,' this 'ethnicizability' had assumed by far the most marked distinction between 'us' and 'them.' Ethnicity became, on the one hand, more and more clearly 'applicable' as exclusionary practice in the daily interaction between 'natives' and 'foreigners' and, on the other hand, became more and more clearly usable as an *explanatory theory* in the participating sciences."

35. Again, this could be regarded as something of an exaggeration, since information on social security benefits, for example, is available in Turkish.

36. Italicized words indicate overlaps in speech between the two speakers.

> Beggar: You are right!
> Passerby: It's no good.
> Beggar: No, it's not good.
> Passerby: Yes.
> Beggar: Turkish man, you?
> Passerby: Yes.
> Beggar: I noticed.
> Passerby: Yes, we've got to help, but . . .
> Beggar: *You don't need* to help me!
> Passerby: Of course + I mean ++ if someone
> Beggar: (particularly abruptly) You're=you're right!

37. Roche (1989) has suggested that the use of *du* by Germans to foreigners is not necessarily condescending and familiar, but merely echoes the foreigners' own use of *du* with colleagues at work. I do not agree with this statement in general, and this is certainly not the case with the present example.

Chapter 4

1. In the following section I draw heavily on Kreuzer and Seibert (1984), Hamm (1988), and Raddatz (1994).

2. At least until African asylum seekers and refugees assumed this position.

3. Katsoulis (1978:59), cited in Hamm (1988:39) ("The special provisions for members of European Community countries in the foreigner law should not conceal the fact that the Federal Republic and the other Community countries have the right to deport or to deny residency to foreigners from EC member states on the grounds of 'public order, security, and health' ").

4. Pazarkaya now lives in Great Britain, however.

5. For a very useful introduction to female foreign writers, see Ackermann (1991).

6. "their irritation in their new, strange surroundings, their confrontation with a foreign society and culture, with methods and conditions of productions that they are not used to and often do not understand, their homesickness, their dreams and hopes, their new sorrows and joys."

7. "to fill the isolation in a foreign country with writing ... or ... to bear witness to the course of one's own life, or to communicate it."

8. "The language they use against this isolation is the language of their immediate surroundings. Surroundings which are colored as much by the memories they brought with them, as by everyday life in a foreign country. This language might be the dialect of the home village, but it is often a very unsophisticated Italian. The place of writing is a room in a hostel or a works apartment, a room in town where, of course, he lives alone."

9. "The emigrants who had decided to stay in Germany also saw themselves confronted with numerous problems. The emigration phenomenon grew more complex. It lost more of its provisional character, and the themes of the early years, such as homesickness, lost their primacy. Life in the new home meant at the same time a confrontation with another culture. That this problem was not to be easily solved was manifest in the fact that the calls to scale the walls of the ghetto soon became loud."

10. "This is the phase in which, in the poems of Biondi, one can read about *Krümmeln* instead of *Krümeln* ('crumbs'), a *runttergehenden Sonne* (cf. *untergehende Sonne*—'setting sun'), or where you find the construction *als wie es normal sei* instead of *als ob es normal sei* ('as if it were normal'). It is also the phase in which Kemal Kurt reminisces in little prose sketches about homemade Turkish poppy-seed syrup, weddings, and melon liqueur—shreds of melancholy, touching, naive. It is not literature."

11. "According to Liverani's foreword, neglecting form issues as opposed to content was in line with the living conditions of migrant workers: Guest worker literature 'on account of the actual reality of the guest worker existence, cannot be based on linguistic niceties or on form....' Such a marginalization of aesthetic problems, asserted to be necessary for the moment, is also a result of and an indicator of the authenticity of this literature.... That those 'affected' are speaking here is stressed time and again; Liverani closes his foreword by noting that what the poems have 'in common' is 'that they are authentically experienced and come directly from under one's own skin.'"

12. Frederking (1985a).

13. Biondi and Schami (1983).

14. "Being affected, which is expressed in this way, is what binds the group together: Turks, Italians, Greeks, and Spaniards are all affected in the same way. This common affectedness assures the group of unity."

15. "the old topic of discussion, based on experienced authenticity, according to which the foreign writer as author has to be a Gastarbeiter who has experienced everything personally and has become a writer on the strength of it."

16. The celebrated Czech writer Libuse Monikova is an extremely interesting case in point. She has been at great pains throughout her career in Germany to be accepted as an academic and intellectual and to distance herself from Gastarbeiter. While she links her immigration to Germany at least vaguely to the Prague Spring, she has been heard to protest in response to

a question about Gastarbeiter with the declaration, "ich weiß nichts von Arbeitern" (reading and discussion, North Carolina State University Student Center, Raleigh, 21 October 1992). While this is a topic for another forum, it is worth noting here that her aversion to being associated with workers appears to me to have had an effect on her writing style. In *Pavane für eine verstorbene Infantin* (1983), for example, she hypercorrects away from Gastarbeiterdeutsch and Gastarbeiterliteratur to such an extent that her style is intensely (perhaps, overly) academic and her erudite allusions almost too densely packed. In her brilliant recent novel, *Die Fassade* (1987), however, while the cultural allusions are still rich and academic, there is in my opinion a new lightness and humor about her style that suggests she has worked through this identity crisis and feels secure as an immigrant academic writing in Germany.

17. "The stigma 'Gastarbeiter' is an advantage here."

18. "The unhappy combination of 'Gastarbeiterdeutsch' and 'affectedness' has led to their being hardly a critical work extant on this literature that makes the effort to make it the object of literary criticism. Literary critics still consider it as twittering for linguists and sociologists."

19. "Just how impertinent is it to use the name 'foreigner literature' for something that has become an integral part of our poetry, prose, and satire? Just how much respect do we owe, rather, to these writers who work masterfully, playfully, and sometimes almost genially with the German language—some of them (like Rafik Schami) already being best-selling authors."

20. Citizenship is possible for third-generation immigrant children under strict regulation (see Chapter 2). We might also note that the federal government has proposed a second category of "German-ness" with immigrant children expressly in mind: while full German citizenship is designated as *Staatsangehörigkeit*, which offers all the rights and privileges, the new category has been labelled *Staatszugehörigkeit*, literally, "belonging to the state," though this does not entail all the other rights of real citizenship.

21. HSM is an anonymous author.

22. "We are not accepted in any society. In the FRG we are guest workers, foreigners, even worse: Turks. In our home countries we are Deutschlanders, Allemani, worse: capitalists."

23. In Ackerman (1984b:23–24) ("In Germany I was a foreigner and in Portugal I was 'the German girl.' Where do I belong?").

24. ANGORA

    Ankara
    Strange to me
    but close

    Out of your arms
    I have grown
    Soon you will have
    me again
    and I

>   will greet you
>   Between us
>   lives
>   open and hidden
>   more than just
>   one life

25. "We talk a mixture, neither proper German nor proper Turkish, Italian, or Greek. We are not at home in any language any more. We are on a futile search for an answer to the question, who we actually are."

26. "Language becomes the point of crystallization. For many foreigners who write it is a symbol of their lack of cultural belonging. . . . Language or more exactly deficient linguistic-expressive ability becomes the marker of ethnic and cultural identity problems."

27. > Before I speak a word
>   I think very carefully
>   I should make no mistake
>   so that I don't stand out
>   in front of such a select audience
>   as an ignorant fool
>   who always behaves badly

28. > You live in two languages,
>   But you command none.
>   One you forget,
>   You misuse the other.

29. LANGUAGE FIELDS

>   In my head
>   the boundaries of two languages have
>   blurred
>   but
>   between me
>   and me
>   still runs
>   the boundary fence
>   which leaves behind wounds
>   every time
>   I open it

30. "And on my brow, on my jacket was written from birth 'Gastarbeiter'; that meant exploitable, without rights, deportable. With this word my fate was sealed with rubber stamp and seal. And someone had invented this word for us and written it down, someone who did not know us, who could appreciate the profit to be made from this word, and who profited from it."

31. "I came to you; you said, first learn German. I learned German and came to you again. You introduced me to the perversions of your language, the jokes about Turks."

32. "Rather, [Gastarbeiter literature] is intended to appeal to those people

who are on the same level as Gastarbeiter, as well as those people who want to learn about how their situation is and how it can develop, in order to understand better. Thereby, they are attempting to write their literature more and more in German. In so doing, they wanted, and still want, to stress the common ground, to build bridges to German citizens and to all the various minorities of different linguistic backgrounds in the Federal Republic."

33. This section is a partly rewritten version of Fennell (1992).

34. I refer the reader again to Mühlhäusler (1984) for a discussion of literary parodies of foreigners speaking German.

35. NOT ONLY GASTARBEITERDEUTSCH

I. the beginnings

mine not good german
i know
i speak
only gastarbeiterdeutsch
and always problems
german people no understand
what i say
what i want
but

slowly slowly
it goes [better]

I now more understand

36. Arguably a regional, rather than a generic feature.

37. For a discussion of eye dialect (nonstandard spellings that are intended to imbue a character with color, rather than register a true linguistic variant), see Bowdre (1971).

38. All of these examples to follow are from Schami (1988), unless otherwise indicated. There are numerous other examples throughout the literature, as a glance in any anthology would verify.

39. In an essay entitled "Die Fremde wohnt in der Sprache," Biondi does admit to having had at one time "einen kleinen Hang zur Linguistik" ("a little penchant for linguistics").

40. "Now, Mr. . . .," the Inspector began.
"Mschiha," he added.
"Well, Mr. Adonis . . ."
"Mudopulos . . . ," the Greek corrected [him] and explained, adding "Adonis is my first name."
"Yes, Mr Monopolos . . ."

41. "A charge hand issues me a time card. . . . He takes exception to my name: 'That's not a name. That's a disease. Nobody can spell that.' I have to spell it out for him a number of times: S-i-g-i-r-l-i-o-g-l-u. But he still writes

it down wrong as 'Sinnlokus' and puts it in place of my given name. My surname is made out of my second given name Levent. 'How can anyone have a name like that!' He does not calm down for a long time, although his own name 'Symanowski' or something like that would present its own problems to a Turk...."

42. Wallraff is, of course, a native speaker of German.

43. "'What's your name? Kerstin?'" "'No, Nesrin!'" "'Nersin, Nesrir, oh, Nesrin!'"

44. The expressions "foreigner" and "Turk" have frequently taken on the same meaning in colloquial speech and can be used for one another at will.

45. Though the term *Türke* would less likely be used for a Japanese or other Asian.

46. This poem by Zachaviera is from an Edition Xylos publication. Edition Xylos is no longer operating in Essen.

> I sit
> in rooms with English furniture,
> drink tea,
> enjoy myself.
> We both know,
> that I am really sitting on a suitcase
> somewhere,
> and build my nest
> between Turks and Greeks.
> Close eyes
> — a sponge,
> dried up with compromises,
> loud clothes
> and superior knowledge.
> Suck up
> a little melancholy and homesickness,
> am disappointed, that only one
> of these Turks and Greeks
> smells of garlic
> and enthusiastically, I want
> to speak to him,
> but he shows me
> silently
> his wallet.

47. Where *fressen* is the general word for "eat" for animals, *essen* is the general word "eat" for humans.

48. Used to refer to an immigrant worker's home.

49. A reviewer informs me that the terms *Schwarze(r)* and *Neger* are not necessarily derogatory and that the term *Mandelauge* can be "flattering." This has not been my experience.

50. There is a difference between language and literature here in that there is no stage corresponding to creolization.

51. UNDERSTAND

   I Turk. No understand!
   I Greek. German no understand!
   I Yugoslav. Not German understand!
   I'm a Spaniard. I not understand German!
   I'm an Italian. I don't understand German well!
   I'm a German. I don't understand any of you!

52. I am the foreigner
    the last filth
    on earth
    am ashamed
    on the street
    in the pub
    in the discotheque
    with my black hair
    black eyes
    black mustache
    and
    dark skin
    by nature stigmatized

    I am the foreigner
    the last filth
    on earth

    No one talks to me
    no one visits me
    I, foreigner,
    no understand, no speak
    I am the foreigner
    the last filth
    on earth

53. My two countries and I
    We are wedded
    Until death do us part
    And now I am here
    Among you
    With you
    And I will not desist from me
    Or from you

54. "When foreign men and women began to write a number of years ago, it was primarily a question of coping with loneliness and isolation and of overcoming negative experiences. Stepping into the public arena made him/her

realize he/she was not alone. Solidarity developed amongst those affected, and access to the German reader, who also had to feel affected, was made easier by their choosing the German language as a vehicle for engaging German reality. When foreign men and women write German today, they do not want only to raise consciousness about being foreign and to ease relationships. They also want to have an influence on the German reality, of which they have become part. They want to offer resistance to laws and regulations which make integration more difficult and promote isolation. They want to take an active part in social, political, and cultural life, and they want to make the decision to stay or to go of their own free will, without being subjected to massive legal and social pressure."

55. "We live on the edge even of the literary society of this country. None of us is given opportunity, for example, to give a guest lecture at the University of Frankfurt on his aesthetics. I should imagine that Biondi or I would be in a position to present the aesthetic bases of our literature on the university level and to subsequently publish it, so that it can be discussed. . . . And this is not appreciated, by any institution, by any press, by anyone."

56. "They do not just bring in foreign words (in the way Zehra Çırak's 'Zufallsfeige' ["accidental smack"] for a father's smack brings in a certain foreign flavor), and they do not just smuggle in unusual cargo like cicadas or musk melons; to make that observation seems to me to border on a wry head-scarf solidarity. Rather, I mean a certain precision with words, an edge, with which syllables, tones, sounds are placed under the microscope, newly perceived and newly acquired (fashioned?)."

57. I give you a dictionary/ you and me/ one us no roof
and in this land/ a house/ chamber
of nothing and word
from word of word
from and –
from language skins/ hoy today
is green is white is snow a window
far so far

I give you my dictionary
not of my foreign land – ojo!
the lonelinesses/ of my skin and
germany, mycountry – you
too and always andland and/ and
german   land out of sight/ land people forgotten
this land is/ . . .

. . . a death like Auschwitz still

no neodeath no neomurder/ no new and neo no/ and Cain:
murder and death stays the same/ says

a death like Auschwitz still?

58. STRANGE DEATH

>Uprooted
>And overgrown with strange death
>I throw myself off
>Night
>By Night
>From myself
>
>Open grave
>My thin skin
>Cold from angry looks
>Penetrates freely
>In and out
>
>Turned backward
>I break off
>Into the coming day

59. "Not only a brilliant, linguistically gifted, and vivid narrator, but also a romancer who cunningly juggles with the tools of modern prose."

60. "But this insistence on 'Gastarbeiterdeutsch' as a literary language is ambivalent, however, since it can signify both deficient mastery of German as well as skillfully productive familiarity with these 'deficiencies.'"

61. See Mühlhäusler (1984) for a brief but useful summary of Germany's colonial activities (or the lack of them).

Bibliography

Ackermann, Irmgard (1991) German literature by female foreigners. Official translation of keynote paper presented at the Symposium on Cultural and Linguistic Diversity—Views of the Other: Minorities within the Setting of Germanic Languages and Literatures, Ohio State University, 15–17 March 1991.
——— (1984a) Integrationsvorstellungen und Integrationsdarstellungen in der Ausländerliteratur. In Kreuzer and Seibert (1984), pp. 23–39.
———, ed. (1984b) *In zwei Sprachen leben: Berichte, Erzählungen, Gedichte von Ausländern.* 2nd edition. Munich: Deutscher Taschenbuch Verlag.
Ackermann, Irmgard, and Harald Weinrich, eds. (1986) *Eine nicht nur deutsche Literatur: Zur Standardbestimmung der "Ausländerliteratur."* Munich and Zürich: Piper.
Adelson, Leslie A. (1990) Migrants' literature or German literature?: TORKAN's *Tufan: Brief an einen islamischen Bruder. German Quarterly* 63 (3/4):382–89.
Aksoy, Fevzi (1975?) *Das Gastarbeiterproblem: Rotation? Integration? Arbeitsplatzverlagerung?* Munich: Eigenverlag der Südosteuropa-Gesellschaft.
Aktion Gemeinsinn (1993) *Die "Ausländer" und wir.* Bonn: Aktion Geimeinsinn.
Aktoprak, Levent (1987) *Unterm Arm die Odysee.* Frankfurt am Main: Dagyeli Verlag.
Alatis, J. E. (1970) *Report of the 20th Annual Round Table Meeting on Linguistics and Language Studies.* Monograph Series on Languages and Linguistics, no. 22. Washington, D.C.: Georgetown University Press.
Andersen, Roger N., ed. (1984) *Second Languages: A Cross-Linguistic Perspective.* Rowley, Mass.: Newbury House.
———, ed. (1983) *Pidginization and Creolization as Language Acquisition.* Rowley, Mass.: Newbury House.
———, ed. (1981a) *New Dimensions in Research on the Acquisition and Use of a Second Language.* Rowley, Mass.: Newbury House.
——— (1981b) Two perspectives on pidginization as second language acquisition. In Andersen (1981a), pp. 165–95.
Auer, J. C. P. (1984) *Bilingual Conversation.* Amsterdam: John Benjamins.
Auer, J. C. P., and A. di Luzio, eds. (1984) *Interpretive Sociolinguistics.* Tübingen: Gunter Narr Verlag.
Bade, Klaus J. (1994) *Ausländer, Aussiedler, Asyl: Eine Bestandaufnahme.* Munich: C. H. Beck.
——— (1983) *Vom Auswanderungsland zum Einwanderungsland: Deutschland 1880–1980.* Berlin: Colloquium.
Barbour, Stephen, and Patrick Stephenson (1990) *Variation in German: A Critical Introduction to German Sociolinguistics.* Cambridge: Cambridge University Press.

Barkowski, Hans, Ulrike Harnisch, and Sigrid Krumm (1976) Sprachhandlungstheorie und "Deutsch für ausländische Arbeiter." *Linguistische Berichte* 45:42–54.
Barth, F., ed. (1969) *Ethnic Groups and Boundaries.* Boston: Little, Brown.
Bektas, Habib, ed. (1980) *Das Unsichtbare sagen!: Prosa und Lyrik aus dem Alltag des Gastarbeiters.* Kiel: Neuer Malik Verlag.
Bereiter, Carl, and Siegfried Engelmann (1966) *Teaching Disadvantaged Children in the Pre-School.* Englewood Cliffs, N.J.: Prentice-Hall.
Bernstein, Basil (1971) *Class, Codes and Control.* Vol. 1. London: Routledge & Kegan Paul.
Bernstein, Cynthia G., ed. (1994) *The Text and Beyond: Essays in Literary Linguistics.* Tuscaloosa: University of Alabama Press.
Bickerton, Derek (1981) Discussion of Andersen (1981b). In Andersen (1981a), pp. 202–6.
Biehle, Jürgen (1987) *Sprachlernbedingungen und Zweitsprachenerwerb türkischer Schüler.* Weinheim: Deutscher Studienverlag.
Biondi, Franco (1991) *Die Unversöhnlichen—Im Labyrinth der Herkunft.* Tübingen: Heliopolis Verlag.
——— (1986) Die Fremde wohnt in der Sprache. In Ackermann and Weinrich (1986), pp. 25–32.
——— (1984) Von den Tränen zu den Bürgerrechten: Ein Einblick in die italienische Emigrantenliteratur. In Kreuzer and Seibert (1984), pp. 75–100.
Biondi, Franco, and Rafik Schami (1983) Ein Gastarbeiter ist ein Türke. *Kürbiskern* 1:94–106.
——— (1981) Literatur der Betroffenheit. In Schaffernicht (1981), pp. 124–36.
Biondi, Franco, Jusuf Naoum, Rafik Schami, and Suleman Taufiq, eds. (1980) *Im neuen Land.* Bremen: Südwind gastarbeiterdeutsch.
Blackshire-Belay, Carol (1991) *Language Contact: Verb Morphology in German of Foreign Workers.* Tübingen: Gunter Narr Verlag.
Blanc, H., M. le Douaron, and D. Véronique, eds. (1987) *Apprendre une langue étrangère.* Paris: Didier.
Bodemann, Y. Michael, and Robin Ostow (1975) Lingua Franca und Pseudo-Pidgin in der Bundesrepublik Deutschland: Fremdarbeiter und Einheimische im Sprachzusammenhang. In Klein (1975), pp. 122–46.
Bourdieu, Pierre (1984) *Distinction: A Social Critique of the Judgement of Taste.* Cambridge, Mass.: Harvard University Press.
——— (1977) *Ce que parler veut dire: L'économie des échanges linguistiques.* Paris: Arthème Fayard.
Bowdre, Paul Hull, Jr. (1971) Eye dialect as a literary device. In Williamson and Burke (1971), pp. 178–86.
Breton, R., and M. Pinard (1960) Group formation among immigrants: Criteria and processes. *Canadian Journal of Economics and Political Science* 26:465–77.
Brown, H. D., ed. (1976) *Papers in Second Language Acquisition. Language Learning,* special issue, 4. Ann Arbor: Research Club on Language Learning.
Brown, R., and A. Gilman (1960) The pronouns of power and solidarity. In Sebeok (1960), pp. 253–76.

Bundesministerium für Jugend, Familie, Frauen und Gesundheit (1989) *Hearing zur Situation ausländischer Frauen und Mädchen aus den Anwerbestaaten.* Parts 1 and 2 (September). Bonn: Bundesministerium für Jugend, Familie, Frauen und Gesundheit.

Bundesministerium für Frauen und Jugend (1992) *Frauen in der Bundesrepublik Deutschland.* (October). Bonn: Bundesministerium für Frauen und Jugend.

Calhoun, Craig, Edward LiPuma, and Moishe Postone, eds. (1993) *Bourdieu: Critical Perspectives.* Chicago: University of Chicago Press.

Candlin, Christopher (1989) General editor's preface. In Fairclough (1989), pp. vi–x.

Castles, Stephen, and Godula Kosack (1985) *Immigrant Workers and Class Structure in Western Europe.* 2nd edition. Oxford: Oxford University Press.

Chiellino, Gino (1985) *Literatur und Identität in der Fremde.* Augsburg: Bürgerhaus Kreßlesmühle.

Clahsen, Harald, Jürgen Meisel, and Horst Pienemann (1983) *Deutsch als Zweitsprache: Der Spracherwerb ausländischer Arbeiter.* Tübingen: Gunter Narr Verlag.

Clahsen, Harald, and Ulrike Rohde (1977) Untersuchungen zur Sprache ausländischer Arbeiter in der BRD. *Studium Linguistik* 1:89–94.

Clyne, Michael (1984) *Language and Society in the German-Speaking Countries.* Cambridge: Cambridge University Press.

——— (1968) Zum Pidgindeutsch der Gastarbeiter. *Zeitschrift für Mundartforschung* 35:130–39.

Collins, James (1993) Determination and contradiction: An appreciation and critique of the work of Pierre Bourdieu on language and education. In Calhoun, LiPuma, and Postone (1993), pp. 116–38.

Cook-Gumperz, Jenny, and John J. Gumperz (1976) Context in children's speech. Papers on Language and Context, working paper no. 46. Berkeley: Language Behavior Research Laboratory, University of California, Berkeley.

Conklin, Nancy Faires, and Margaret A. Lourie (1983) *A Host of Tongues: Language Communities in the United States.* New York: The Free Press.

Corder, S. P. and E. Roulet, eds. (1977) *The Notions of Simplification, Interlanguages and Pidgins and their Relation to Second Language Pedagogy: Actes du 5ème Colloque de linguistique appliquée à Neuchâtel, 20–22 May 1976.* Liebefeld and Bern: Langdruck.

Corson, D. (1993) *Language, Minority Education and Gender: Linking Social Justice and Power.* Clevedon, Philadelphia, and Adelaide: Multilingual Matters.

De Laurentiis, Allegra (1985) Einige Gedanken über die generationsbedingte Sprachlernfähigkeit von Arbeitsmigranten. *Zielsprache Deutsch* 2:2–6.

di Luzio, A. (1984) On the meaning of language choice for the sociocultural identity of migrant children. In Auer and di Luzio (1984), pp. 55–85.

Dittmar, Norbert (1989) La sémantique en construction. *Langage et société* 51: 39–66.

——— (1984) Semantic features of pidginized learner varieties of German. In Andersen (1984), pp. 243–70.

——— (1979) Zum Nutzen von Ergebnissen der Untersuchung des ungesteuerten Zweitspracherwerbs ausländischer Kinder. In Kloepfer (1979), pp. 371-96.

——— (1973) *Soziolinguistik: Exemplarische und kritische Darstellung ihrer Theorie, Empirie und Anwendung.* Frankfurt am Main: Athenäum Verlag.

Dittmar, Norbert, and H. Kuhberg (1988) Der Vergleich temporaler Ausdrucksmittel in der Zweitsprache Deutsch in Lernervarietäten zweier elfjähriger Kinder mit den Ausgangssprachen Polnisch und Türkisch anhand von Longitudinaldaten. In Vater and Erich (1988), pp. 308-29.

Dittmar, Norbert, and Astrid Reich (1987) Référence spatiale dans les variétés d'apprenant de quatre migrants polonais en allemand L2. In Blanc, Le Douaron, and Véronique (1987), pp. 155-68.

Dittmar, Norbert, A. Reich, M. Schumacher, R. Skiba, and H. Terborg (1988) *Modalität von Lernervarietäten im Langschnitt—Die Erlernung modaler Konzepte des Deutschen durch erwachsene polnische Migranten: Eine empirische Langschnittstudie.* Berliner Papiere zum Zweitsprachenerwerb: Projekt P-MoLL. Berlin: Freie Universität Berlin.

Dittmar, Norbert, and Christiane von Stutterheim (1985) On the discourse of immigrant workers: Interethnic communication and communication strategies. In Van Dijk (1985), pp. 125-52.

——— (1984) Communication strategies of migrants in interethnic interaction. In Auer and di Luzio (1984), pp. 179-214.

Dittrich, Eckhard J., and Frank-Olaf Radtke, eds. (1990) *Ethnizität.* Opladen: Westdeutscher Verlag.

Dulay, Heidi, Marina Burt, and Stephen Krashen (1982) *Language Two.* New York: Oxford University Press.

Ebneter, Theodor (1976) *Angewandte Linguistik: Eine Einführung.* 2 vols. Munich: Fink.

Edwards, John R. (1985) *Language, Society and Identity.* Oxford: Blackwell.

———, ed. (1984) *Linguistic Minorities, Policies and Pluralism.* London and New York: Academic Press.

——— (1977) Ethnic identity and bilingual education. In Giles (1977), pp. 253-82.

Ejerhed, Eva, and Inger Henrysson, eds. (1981) *Tvåspråkighet.* Acta Universitatis Umensis, 36. Umeå: GOTAB AB.

Esselborn, Karl, ed. (1987) *Über Grenzen: Berichte, Erzählungen, Gedichte von Ausländern.* Munich: Deutscher Taschenbuch Verlag.

Fairclough, Norman, ed. (1992) *Critical Language Awareness.* London and New York: Longman.

——— (1989) *Language and Power.* London and New York: Longman.

Fennell, Barbara A. (1994) Literary data and linguistic analysis: The example of Modern German immigrant worker literature. In Bernstein (1994), pp. 241-62.

——— (1992) Markers of ethnic identity in Immigrant Worker German. *Language Quarterly* 30 (1-2): 1-19.

——— (1991) Investigating the semantic reconstruction of Immigrant Worker German. Paper presented at the Symposium on Cultural and Linguistic

Diversity—Views of the Other: Minorities within the Setting of Germanic Languages and Literatures, Ohio State University, 15-17 March 1991.

——— (1989) Now you see it, now you don't: Pidgin and creole characteristics of Immigrant Worker German in the Federal Republic. Paper presented at NWAVE 18, Duke University, October 1989.

——— (1988) Sociolinguistic theory and literary analysis. Paper presented at the Twentieth Anniversary Conference of the Southeast Conference on Linguistics, Norfolk, Va., October 1988.

Ferguson, Charles F. (1959) Diglossia. *Word* 15:325-40.

——— (1977) Simplified registers, broken language, Gastarbeiterdeutsch. In Molony, Zobl, and Stölting (1977), pp. 25-39.

——— (1971) Absence of copula and the notion of simplicity: A study of normal speech, baby talk, foreigner talk and pidgins. In Hymes (1971), pp. 141-45.

Fishman, J., ed. (1968) *Readings in the Sociology of Language.* The Hague: Mouton.

——— (1977) Language and ethnicity. In Giles (1977), pp. 15-52.

Foley, William A. (1988) Language birth: The process of pidginization and creolization. In Newmeyer (1988), pp. 162-83.

Fox, Anthony (1990) *The Structure of German.* Oxford: Clarendon Press.

Franzen, J. (1978) *Gastarbeiter—Raumrelevante Verhaltensweisen: Migrationsmodell und empirische Studie am Beispiel jugoslawischer Arbeitskräfte in Hannover.* Hannover: Geographische Gesellschaft zu Hannover.

Frederking, Monika (1985a) *Schreiben gegen Vorurteile: Literatur türkischer Migranten in der Bundesrepublik Deutschland.* Berlin: Express-Edition.

——— (1985b) Zweisprachigkeit bei türkischen Kindern in der Bundesrepublik Deutschland. *Zielsprache Deutsch* 3:18-25.

Friedrich, Heinz, ed. (1986) *Chamisso's Enkel: Literatur von Ausländern in Deutschland.* Munich: Deutscher Taschenbuch Verlag.

Gal, Susan (1987) Codeswitching and consciousness in the European periphery. *American Ethnologist* 14:637-53.

Gehlen, Norbert, Wolfgang Jung, Carola Kurras, Guido Schmitt, amd Wolfgang Schwark (1977) Freiburger Forschungsprojekt: Schulische und außerschulische Sozialisation ausländischer Arbeiterkinder. *Deutsch Lernen* 1:32-41.

Giambusso, Giuseppe, ed. (1982) *Wurzeln, hier: Gedichte italienischer Emigranten/Le radici, qui: Poesie di emigrati italiani.* Bremen: Edition Cohn.

Gilbert, Glenn G. (1983) Transfer in second language acquisition. In Andersen (1983), pp. 168-80.

Giles, Howard (1979) Ethnicity markers in speech. In Scherer and Giles (1979), pp. 251-90.

———, ed. (1977) *Language, Ethnicity and Intergroup Relations.* New York: Academic Press.

Giles, Howard, and P. M. Smith (1979) Accommodation theory: Optimal levels of convergence. In Giles and St. Clair (1979), pp. 45-65.

Bibliography

Giles, Howard, and R. N. St. Clair, eds. (1979) *Language and Social Psychology*. Oxford: Blackwell.

Glaser, D. (1958) Dynamics of ethnic identification. *American Sociological Review* 23:31-40.

Goffman, E. (1955) On face-work: An analysis of ritual elements in social interaction. *Psychiatry* 19:213-31.

Götze, Lutz (1987) Muttersprachlicher Unterricht—Seine Bedeutung für den ausländischen Schüler, sein Stellenwert in der deutschen Schule. *Zielsprache Deutsch* 2:20-25.

Greenberg, J., S. L. Kirkland, and T. Pyszczynski (1988) Some theoretical notions and preliminary research concerning derogatory ethnic labels. In Smitherman-Donaldson and Van Dijk (1988), pp. 74-92.

Grosch, Klaus (1992) Foreigners and aliens. In Stern (1992), pp. 132-51.

Hamm, Horst (1988) *Fremdgegangen—freigeschrieben: Eine Einführung in die deutschsprachige Gastarbeiterliteratur*. Würzburg: Königshausen und Neumann.

Hancock, I. F. (1977) Repertory of pidgin and creole languages. In Valdman (1977), pp. 362-91.

Hatch, Evelyn, ed. (1978) *Second Language Acquisition: A Book of Readings*. Rowley, Mass.: Newbury House.

Heidelberger Forschungsprojekt "Pidgin-Deutsch" (1975) Zur Sprache ausländischer Arbeiter: Syntaktische Analysen und Aspekte des kommunikativen Verhaltens. In Klein (1975), pp. 78-121.

Henne, Helmut (1986) *Jugend und ihre Sprache: Darstellung, Materialien, Kritik*. Berlin: Walter de Gruyter.

Herbert, Ulrich (1990) *A History of Foreign Labor in Germany, 1880-1980: Seasonal Workers, Forced Laborers, Guest Workers*. Ann Arbor: University of Michigan Press.

Herrmann, Helga (1995) Ausländische Jugendliche in Ausbildung und Beruf. *Aus Politik und Zeitgeschichte* (insert in the weekly newspaper *Das Parlament*). 25 August 1995:23-29.

Hexelschneider, Erhard (1989) Daheim in der Fremde. *Muttersprache* 99(4): 349-55.

Hinnenkamp, Volker (1990) "Gastarbeiterlinguistik" und die Ethnisierung der Gastarbeiter. In Dittrich and Radtke (1990), pp. 277-98.

——— (1989) *Interaktionale Soziolinguistik und Interkulturelle Kommunikation: Gesprächsmanagement zwischen Deutschen und Türken*. Tübingen: Niemeyer.

——— (1984) Eye-witnessing pidginization: Structural and sociolinguistic aspects of German and Turkish foreigner talk. *York Papers in Linguistics* 2: 153-66.

——— (1982) *Foreigner Talk und Tarzanisch*. Hamburg: Buske Verlag.

Hoffmann, Charlotte (1991) *An Introduction to Bilingualism*. London: Longman.

Hoffmann, Lutz, and Herbert Even (1984) *Soziologie der Ausländerfeindlichkeit: Zwischen nationaler Identität und multikultureller Gesellschaft*. Weinheim and Basel: Beltz Verlag.

Holm, John (1988-89) *Pidgins and Creoles*. 2 vols. Cambridge: Cambridge University Press.

Horn, Dieter (1986) Schreiben aus Betroffenheit—Die Migrantenliteratur in der Bundesrepublik. In Tumat (1986), pp. 213-33.

Hyltenstam, Kenneth, and K. Maandi, eds. (1984) *Nordens språk som målspråk*. Stockholm: Institute of Linguistics, Stockholm University.

Hymes, D., ed. (1971) *Pidginization and Creolization of Languages*. Cambridge: Cambridge University Press.

James, Carl (1980) *Contrastive Analysis*. Cambridge: Cambridge University Press.

Jones, Philip (1983) Guestworkers and their spatial distribution. In Wild (1983), pp. 71-107.

Karasholi, Adel (1992) *Wenn Damaskus nicht wäre: Gedichte*. Munich: A1 Informationen Gesellschaft.

Katsoulis, Haris (1984) *Bürger zweiter Klasse: Ausländer in der Bundesrepublik*. 2nd edition. Bonn: Express Edition.

Keim, Inken (1984) *Untersuchungen zum Deutsch türkischer Gastarbeiter*. Tübingen: Gunter Narr Verlag.

—— (1978) *Gastarbeiterdeutsch*. Forschungsbericht des Instituts für Deutsche Sprache, no. 41. Tübingen: Gunter Narr Verlag.

Klein, Wolfgang (1986) *Second Language Acquisition*. Cambridge: Cambridge University Press.

——, ed. (1975) *Sprache ausländischer Arbeiter. Zeitschrift für Literaturwissenschaft und Linguistik*, Heft 18. Göttingen: Vandenhoeck und Ruprecht.

Klein, Wolfgang, and Clive Perdue (1992) *Utterance Structure: Developing Grammars Again*. Amsterdam and Philadelphia: John Benjamins.

Klein, Wolfgang, and Norbert Dittmar (1979) *Developing Grammars: The Acquisition of German Syntax by Foreign Workers*. Berlin: Springer-Verlag.

Kloepfer, Rolf, ed. (1979) *Bildung und Ausbildung in der Romania*. Munich: Fink.

Kolodny, E. (1977) *Les étrangers à Stuttgart*. Paris: Centre Nationale de la Recherche Scientifique.

Kotsinas, Ulla-Britt (1991) *Invandrare talar svenska*. Edsbruk: Akademitryck.

—— (1988) Immigrant children's Swedish—A new variety? *Journal of Multilingual and Multicultural Development* 9 (1-2):129-40.

—— (1984a) "Vad heter stan på din mamma?": Om prepositionsanvändningen i några invandrares svenska talspråk. In Hyltenstam and Maandi (1984), pp. 188-203.

—— (1984b) Semantic overextension and lexical overuse in immigrant Swedish. *Scandinavian Working Papers on Bilingualism* 2:23-42. Stockholm: University of Stockholm Institute of Linguistics.

—— (1982) "Kommer en papper på kyrka?": Lokativa prepositioner i invandrarsvenska. In *Svenskans beskrivning 13*, 183-98. Meddelanden från institutionen för nordiska språk och nordisk litteratur vid Helsingfors universitet, series B, 6. Helsinki: Helsinki University.

—— (1981) Kommer och predikatet GÅ: Funderingar kring tempus och aspekt i invandrarsvenska. In Ejerhed and Henrysson (1981), pp. 201-13.

Krejci, J., and V. Velimsky (1981) *Ethnic and Political Nations in Europe*. New York: St. Martin's Press.
Kreuzer, Helmut (1984) Gastarbeiterliteratur, Ausländerliteratur, Migranten- Literatur?: Zur Einführung. In Kreuzer and Seibert (1984), 7–11.
Kreuzer, Helmut, and Peter Seibert, eds. (1984) *Gastarbeiterliteratur. Zeitschrift für Literaturwissenschaft und Linguistik*, Heft 56. Göttingen: Vandenhoeck und Ruprecht.
Kuhberg, H. (1986) *Der Erwerb der Temporalität des Deutschen durch zwei elfjährige Kinder mit Ausgangssprache Türkisch und Polnisch: Eine Longitudinaluntersuchung*. Frankfurt am Main: Peter Lang.
Kummer, Werner (1990) Sprache und kulturelle Identität. In Dittrich and Radtke (1990), pp. 265–75.
Kurz, Claudia (forthcoming) The use of prepositions, articles and simplification in contact varieties of German. *SALSA III: Proceedings of the Third Annual Symposium about Language and Society, Austin*. Austin: University of Texas.
Kutsch, Stefan, and Ilse Desgranges (1985) *Zweitsprache Deutsch—ungesteuerter Erwerb*. Tübingen: Gunter Narr Verlag.
Labov, William (1994) *Principles of Linguistic Change: Internal Factors*. Oxford: Blackwell.
——— (1972) *Sociolinguistic Patterns*. Philadelphia: University of Pennsylvania Press.
——— (1970) The logic of nonstandard English. In Alatis (1970), pp. 1–43.
LePage, R. B., and A. Tabouret-Keller (1985) *Acts of Identity*. Cambridge: Cambridge University Press.
Lewandowski, T. (1976) *Linguistisches Wörterbuch*. 3 vols. 2nd edition. Heidelberg: Quelle und Meyer.
Lichtenberger, E. (1984) *Gastarbeiter: Leben in zwei Gesellschaften*. Vienna: Böhlau.
Liverani, Franco [alias Franco Biondi] (1982) Vorwort. In Giambusso (1982), pp. 1–4.
Löffler, H. (1975) *Germanistische Soziolinguistik*. Berlin: Erich Schmidt.
Mahler, Gerhart (1974) *Zweitsprache Deutsch—Die Schulbildung der Kinder ausländischer Arbeitnehmer: Eine Darstellung anhand der Entwicklung in Bayern*. Donauwörth: Auer.
Malchow, Barbara, Keyumars Tayebi, and Ulrike Brand (1990) *Die fremden Deutschen: Aussiedler in der Bundesrepublik*. Reinbek: Rowohlt.
Meier-Braun, Karl-Heinz (1995) 40 Jahre "Gastarbeiter" und Ausländerpolitik in Deutschland. *Aus Politik und Zeitgeschichte* (insert in the weekly newspaper *Das Parlament*). 25 August 1995:14–22.
——— (1992) Deutschland braucht Einwanderer. *Zeitschrift für Kulturaustausch* 2:225–27.
Meisel, Jürgen M. (1983) Strategies of second language acquisition: More than one kind of simplification. In Andersen (1983), pp. 120–57.
——— (1977) Linguistic simplification: A study of immigrant workers' speech and foreigner talk. In Corder and Roulet (1977), pp. 88–113.

―――― (1975a) Ausländerdeutsch und Deutsch ausländischer Arbeiter: Zur möglichen Entstehung eines Pidgin in der BRD. In Klein (1975), pp. 9-53.

―――― (1975b) Der Erwerb des Deutschen durch ausländische Arbeiter: Untersuchungen am Beispiel von Arbeitern aus Italien, Spanien und Portugal. *Linguistische Berichte* 38:59-69.

Meyer-Ingwersen, Johannes (1975) Einige typische Deutschfehler bei türkischen Schülern. In Klein (1975), pp. 68-77.

Milroy, Lesley (1987) *Language and Social Networks*. 2nd edition. Oxford: Blackwell.

Molony, C., H. Zobl, and W. Stölting, eds. (1977) *Deutsch in Kontakt mit anderen Sprachen*. Kronberg/Ts: Scriptor Verlag.

Morgan, Marcyliena, ed. (1994) *The Social Construction of Identity in Creole Situations*. CAAS Special Publication Series, vol. 10. Los Angeles: Center for Afro-American Studies, University of California, Los Angeles.

Mufwene, Salikoko (1994) On decreolization: The case of Gullah. In Morgan (1994), pp. 63-99.

Mühlhäusler, Peter (1984) Tracing the roots of Pidgin German. *Language and Communication* 4(1):27-57.

―――― (1986) *Pidgin and Creole Linguistics*. Oxford: Blackwell.

Newmeyer, Frederick J., ed. (1988) *Language: The Socio-Cultural Context*. Linguistics: The Cambridge Survey, vol. 4. Cambridge: Cambridge University Press.

Ney, Norbert, ed. (1984) *Sie haben mich zu einem Ausländer gemacht . . . Ich bin einer geworden: Ausländer schreiben vom Leben bei uns*. Reinbek: Rowohlt.

Orlovic-Schwarzwald, M. (1978) *Zum Gastarbeiterdeutsch jugoslawischer Arbeiter im Rhein-Main Gebiet: Empirishche Untersuchungen zur Morphologie und zum ungesteuerten Erwerb des Deutschen durch Erwachsense*. Mainzer Studien zur Sprach- und Volksforschung, 2. Wiesbaden: Steiner.

Özakin, Aysel. (1985a) *Du bist willkommen*. Hamburg: Buntbuch-Verlag.

Özkan, Hülya, and Andrea Wörle, eds. (1985) *Eine Fremde wie ich: Berichte, Erzählungen, Gedichte von Ausländerinnen*. Munich: Deutscher Taschenbuch Verlag.

Paulston, Christina Bratt (1974) Questions concerning bilingual education. Paper presented at the Interamerican Conference on Bilingual Education, 1974.

Pavlou, Pavlos, and Glenn G. Gilbert (1991) Gastarbeiterdeutsch (Foreign Workers' German)—An industrial pidgin. Paper presented at the Symposium on Cultural and Linguistic Diversity—Views of the Other: Minorities within the Setting of Germanic Languages and Literatures, Ohio State University, 15-17 March 1991.

Pazarkaya, Yüksel (1984) Türkiye, Mutterland—Almanya, Bitterland . . . Das Phänomen der türkischen Migration als Thema der Literatur. In Kreuzer and Seibert (1984), pp. 101-24.

Pfaff, C. W. (1979) A sociolinguistic framework for research on incipient creolization in "Gastarbeiterdeutsch". Paper presented at the Conference on Theoretical Orientations in Creole Studies, St. Thomas.

Pommerin, Gabriele (1984) *Migrantenliteratur* und ihre Bedeutung für die interkulturelle Erziehung. *Zielsprache Deutsch* 3:41–49.
Raddatz, Fritz J. (1994) In mir zwei Welten. *Die Zeit*, 24 June 1994:45–46.
Raitz, Walter (1989) Einfache Strukturen, deutliche Worte: Zur Poetik der "Gastarbeiterliteratur." *Muttersprache* 99(4):289–98.
Roche, Jörg (1989) *Xenolekt: Struktur und Variation im Deutsch gegenüber Ausländer.* Soziolinguistik und Sprachkontakt, vol. 5. Berlin and New York: Walter de Gruyter.
Romaine, Suzanne (1988) *Pidgin and Creole Languages*. London: Longman.
Rückblick auf die Ausländerbeschäftigung nach 1900: Bericht der Beauftragten der Bundesregierung für die Integration der ausländischen Arbeitnehmer und ihrer Familienangehörigen. September 1986. Bonn.
Saltarelli, M. (1983) L'italiano d'emigrazione: Descrizione, acquisitione ed evoluzione. In *L'italiano come lingua seconda in Italia all'estero*, pp. 401–10. Rome: Ministeri Affari Esteri e Publicca Istruzione.
Saville-Troike, Muriel (1989) *The Ethnography of Communication*. 2nd edition. Oxford: Blackwell.
Schaffernicht, Christian, ed. (1981) *Zu Hause in der Fremde*. Fischerhude: Verlag Atelier im Bauernhaus.
Schami, Rafik (1988) *Die Sehnsucht fährt schwarz: Geschichten aus der Fremde*. Munich: Deutscher Taschenbuch Verlag.
Scherer, Klaus R., and Howard Giles, eds. (1979) *Social Markers in Speech*. London and Cambridge: Cambridge University Press.
Scheron, Bodo, and Ursula Scheron (1982) *Integration von Gastarbeiterkindern*. Frankfurt am Main: Peter Lang.
Scheuer, Helmut (1984) Der "Gastarbeiter" in Literatur, Film und Lied deutscher Autoren. In Kreuzer and Seibert (1984), pp. 62–74.
Schierloh, Heimke (1984) *Das alles für ein Stück Brot: Migrantenliteratur als Objektivierung des "Gastarbeiterdaseins."* Frankfurt am Main: Peter Lang.
Schlobinski, P., G. Kohl, and I. Luding (1993) *Jugendsprache—Fiktion und Wirklichkeit*. Opladen: Westdeutscher Verlag.
Schumann, John (1976) Social distance as a factor in second language acquisition. *Language Learning* 26(1):135–43.
Sebeok, T. A. (1978) *The Pidginization Process: A Model For Second Language Acquisition*. Rowley, Mass.: Newbury House.
———, ed. (1960) *Style in Language*. Boston: M.I.T. Press.
Seibert, Peter (1984) Zur "Rettung der Zungen": Ausländerliteratur in ihren konzeptionellen Ansätzen. In Kreuzer and Seibert (1984), pp. 40–61.
Selinker, Larry (1992) *Rediscovering Interlanguage*. London and New York: Longman.
——— (1972) Interlanguage. *International Review of Applied Linguistics* 10: 209–31.
Shibutani, T. and K. Kwan (1965) *Ethnic Stratification*. New York: Macmillan.
Sivrikozoglu, Çiçek (1985) *. . . nix unsere Vaterland: Zweitsprache Deutsch und soziale Integration*. Werkstattreihe Deutsch als Fremdsprache, vol. 14. Frankfurt am Main: Peter Lang.

Skutnabb-Kangas, T. (1990) *Language, Literacy and Minorities*. London: The Minority Rights Group.
—— (1986) *Minoritet, språk och rasism*. Stockholm and Malmö: Liber.
—— (1984) Children of guest workers and immigrants: Linguistic and educational issues. In Edwards (1984), pp. 17–48.
—— (1981a) Gästarbetare eller invandrare—en jämförelse. In Ejerhed and Henrysson (1981), pp. 111–23.
—— (1981b) Guest worker or immigrant—Different ways of reproducing an underclass. *Journal of Multilingual and Multicultural Development* 2(2):89–115.
Skutnabb-Kangas, T., and P. Toukomaa (1976) *Teaching Migrant Children's Mother Tongue and Learning the Language of the Host Country in the Context of the Socio-Cultural Situation of the Migrant Family*. Research Report 15 (prepared for UNESCO). Tampere: Department of Sociology and Social Psychology, University of Tampere.
Smith, David M. (1972) Some implications for the social status of pidgin languages. In Smith and Shuy (1972), pp. 47–56.
Smith, David M., and Roger Shuy, eds. (1972) *Sociolinguistics in Cross-Cultural Analysis*. Washington, D.C.: Georgetown University Press.
Smitherman-Donaldson, Geneva, and Teun A. van Dijk (1988) *Discourse and Discrimination*. Detroit: Wayne State University Press.
Steinmüller, Ulrich (1983) Förderung des Zweitsprachenerwerbs ausländischer Kinder. *Zielsprache Deutsch* 3:37–48.
—— (1991) Migration and bilingualism. Paper presented at the Symposium on Cultural and Linguistic Diversity—Views of the Other: Minorities within the Setting of Germanic Languages and Literatures, Ohio State University, 15–17 March 1991.
Stern, Susan, ed. (1992) *Meet United Germany*. Frankfurt am Main: Frankfurter Allgemeine Zeitung GmbH Information Services/Atlantik-Brücke.
Stölting, W. (1973) Der serbokroatisch-deutsche Bilingualismus jugoslawischer Schüler in Essen. *Linguistische Berichte* 27:72–81.
Stutterheim, C. von. (1986) *Temporalität in der Zweitsprache*. Berlin and New York: Walter de Gruyter.
Tarone, E., U. Frauenfelder, and L. Selinker (1976) Systematicity/variability and stability/instability in interlanguage systems: More data from Toronto French immersion. In Brown (1976), pp. 93–134.
Taufiq, Suleman, ed. (1983) *Dies ist nicht die Welt, die wir suchen: Ausländer in Deutschland*. Essen: Klartext-Verlag.
Thränhardt, Dietrich (1995) Die Lebenslage der ausländischen Bevölkerung in der Bundesrepublik Deutschland. *Aus Politik und Zeitgeschichte* (insert in the weekly newspaper *Das Parlament*). 25 August 1995:14–22.
Tumat, Alfred J., ed. (1986) *Migration und Integration: Ein Reader* Baltmannsweiler: Schneider Verlag Hohengehren.
Üçüncü, Sadi (1984) *Integrationshemmender Faktor: Ausländerfeindlichkeit in der Bundesrepublik Deutschland, ein Überblick zur Theorie der Ausländerfeindlichkeit*. Pfaffenweiler: Centaurus-Verlagsgesellschaft.

Valdman, A., ed. (1977) *Pidgin and Creole Linguistics*. Bloomington: Indiana University Press.
Van Dijk, Teun, ed. (1985) *Handbook of Discourse Analysis*. Discourse Analysis in Society, vol. 4. New York: Academic Press.
Vater, H., and V. Ullmer-Ehrich, eds. (1988) *Temporalsemantik*. Tübingen: Niemeyer.
Verdoodt, A. (1977) Educational policies on languages: The case of the children of migrant workers. In Giles (1977), 241–53.
Wallraff, Günter (1985) *Ganz unten*. Cologne: Kiepenheuer & Witsch.
────── (1970) *Industriereportagen*. Hamburg: Rowohlt.
Weber, M. (1968). *Economy and Society*. New York: Bedminster.
Whinnom, K. (1971) Linguistic hybridization and the special case of pidgins and creoles. In Hymes (1971), pp. 91–115.
Wild, Trevor, ed. (1983) *Urban and Rural Change in West Germany*. London and Canberra: Croom Helm.
Williamson, Juanita V., and Virginia M. Burke, eds. (1971). *A Various Language: Perspectives on American Dialects*. New York: Holt, Rinehart and Winston.
Wode, H. (1978) Developmental sequences in naturalistic L2 acquisition. In Hatch (1978), pp. 101–17.
Wolfram, Walt, and Natalie Schilling-Estes (1994) *The Ocracoke Brogue: History and Description*. Raleigh: North Carolina Language and Life Project, North Carolina State University and Ocracoke Preservation Society.
────── (1995) Moribund dialects and the endangerment canon: The case of the Ocracoke brogue. *Language* 71:696–721.
Zacharieva, Rumjana (1979) *Fegefeuer: Gedichtensammlung*. Gelsenkirchen: Edition Xylos.

Index

Abate, Carmine, 97
Adalbert von Chamisso Prize, 4, 96, 99, 104
African American (Vernacular) English, 3, 8, 80, 142 (n. 21)
African workers, 28
Agaoglu, Adalet, 99
Aktoprak, Levent, 99, 112
Algerian workers, 28
Anwerbephase, 16–21
Anwerbestopp, 22, 24, 39, 102
Article 16 of the Basic Law, 24, 25
Asylum seekers, 1, 24, 30, 49, 139 (n. 6), 144 (n. 2)
Atacan, Ihsan, 99
Ausländerbeauftragte(r), 22, 23
Ausländerfeindlichkeit, 5, 24, 26, 28–29, 45–50, 103
Ausländergesetz, 20, 24; and writers, 98, 100, 144 (n. 3)
Aussiedler, 29–30
Australia: as immigration country, 12, 83
Austrian Galicia, 13

Bauer, Otto, 133–34
Baykurt, Fakir, 99
Belgian workers, 14, 19
Berlin: Free University of, 3; Wall and influx of workers, 17; and citizenship, 32; Kreuzberg, 78
Bernstein, Basil, 75
Bilingualism, 4; Swedish-Finnish, 75–76
Birthrate: in eastern Germany, 34
Bourdieu, Pierre, 8, 10, 12, 95, 103, 105, 132–37

Canada: as immigration country, 12
Canon, 9; "wars" in United States, 10–11
Capital, 8, 9, 10, 103; literature as, 132–37
CDU-CSU-FDP coalition, 23
Çirak, Zehra, 99, 100
Citizenship, 30–34; Hamburg and, 32; Munich and, 32

Classification struggles, 8–9, 12, 105–37 passim
Consolidation phase. See *Konsolidierungsphase*
Continuum: dialect, 57; creole, 81–83
Creole, 4, 10, 51–93 passim
Creoloid, 77
Cuban workers, 28

D'Adamo, Vito, 97
Dal, Guney, 99, 100
Deficit hypothesis, 75, 143 (n. 34)
Denizeri, Birol, 114
Dialect continuum, 57
Dikmen, Sinasi, 100
Dutch workers, 19

East Germany. See German Democratic Republic
Economic miracle. See *Wirtschaftswunder*
Education, 39–42; deficit in foreign children, 40, 41; qualifications, 40–41
Einwanderungsland, 1, 2, 9, 12, 18, 136
Employment: types, 19, 43; opportunities, 42–45; promotion and, 44
Ethnicity: definitions of, 109–11
Ethnicization of foreign workers, 8, 10, 52, 90–93, 114, 144 (n. 34)
Ethnonyms, 121–24
European Community: freedom of movement in, 1

Familiennachzug, 22
FDP, 24
Fichte, Johann Gottlieb, 4
Filip, Ota, 107
First-generation immigrants: and language, 72; and literature, 111, 114
Forced labor, 15
Foreigners law. See *Ausländergesetz*
Foreigner talk, 53, 142 (nn. 15, 20)
Foreign labor: recruitment, 13
Foreign women, 22, 142 (n. 16); and employment, 45

Index

Foreign Worker German, 3, 10, 104, 107, 111, 146 (n. 18), 152 (n. 60); universal features, 51, 52; and fossilization, 52, 62; typical features of, 54–55; and simplification, 56, 65, 70–72; and pidginization, 65, 68; in past ten years, 84–108; ethnic variants, 115–21
Foreign worker literature, 6, 10, 94–137 passim, 147–48 (n. 32); terms for, 94, 105; *Authentische Literatur*, 105–6; *Literatur der Betroffenheit*, 106–7; developmental nature, 124–32
Foreign workers: terms for, 2, 46; working conditions, 17; population of various nationalities, 19; as new underclass, 20, 46; living conditions, 36–38
France: and problems with foreigners, 49
French workers, 19

Gahse, Zsuzsanna, 101, 105
Gastarbeiterdeutsch. See Foreign Worker German
Gastarbeiterlinguistik, 3, 10, 51; changes in, 84–90
Gastarbeiterliteratur. See Foreign worker literature
Gastarbeiterthematik, 10, 107
German Democratic Republic: foreign workers in, 27–29; and abortion rates, 33–34; and competition for jobs, 41
Great Britain: and problems with foreigners, 49
Greek workers, 19
Gullah, 81–83

Habitus, 10, 11
Heidelberger Forschungsprojekt Pidgindeutsch, 3, 6, 52, 58–62, 85
Herder, Johann Gottfried, 4
Hitler, Adolf, 24
Household structure, 38
Housing, 17, 35; effects on language learning, 68
Hoyerswerda, 29, 49, 136
Hungarian workers, 28

Immigration: historical and political background, 12–34; de facto, 50
Immigration country. See *Einwanderungsland*

Immigration policy, 2, 16, 30; changes in, 22–24
Institut für Deutsch als Fremdsprache, 4, 103
Integration, 18, 35, 36; in schools, 39
Interlanguage, 69–72, 77, 142 (n. 17)
Italian workers, 19
Italian writers, 97–98
Ius sanguinis, 30, 33
Ius solis, 32

Jugendsprache, 80

Kamenko, Vera, 100
Kim Lan Thai, 101
Konsolidierungsphase, 16, 21–22

Ladaki, Fotina, 101
Language transfer, 57
Latin America, 21
Learner dialect, 4, 7, 10, 51–93 passim; in adults, 7

Martha's Vineyard, 83
Matsubara, Hisako, 101
Mölln, 32, 49, 136
Monikova, Libuse, 101, 107, 132
Moslem girls, 41

Naoum, Jusuf, 100
Nazis, 45–46; attitudes to foreign laborers, 15
NPD (National Democratic Party of Germany), 48

Ören, Aras, 96, 99, 100
Outer Banks English, 83
Özakin, Aysel, 96, 99, 100

Pendelkinder, 39
Pidgin, 4, 10, 51–93 passim; and creole studies, 6, 7; varieties of, 64, 66–67
Pidgindeutsch, 52, 64–69
Pirinçci, Akif, 99, 132
Polish, 139 (n. 1); and German prepositional usage, 86–89
Polish workers, 13, 14, 30; in GDR, 28
Portugal, 21

Racial tensions. See *Ausländerfeindlichkeit*
Rajcic, Dragica, 100
Recruitment: contracts, 17. See also *Anwerbephase*; *Anwerbestopp*
Refugees, 1, 24, 30, 49, 144 (n. 2)
Republikaner, 48–49
Reunification, 5, 6, 28, 35, 136
Rinkeby Swedish, 78–81
Rostock-Lichtenhagen, 29, 49
Rotation principle, 18, 24
Rückkehrbereitschaft, 23
Ruhr miners, 13
Russian workers, 14

SAID (Iranian poet), 100, 107
Schäuble, Wolfgang, 23–24
Scheinhardt, Saliha, 100
Second-generation immigrants, 3, 4, 42, 142 (n. 19), 143 (n. 26); and creolization, 72–77; and semilingualism, 74–76; and literature, 111
SED, 29
Seiteneinsteiger, 39
Semilingualism, 3, 74–76
Senoçak, Zafir, 99, 130
Social conditions: improvements in, 35
Solingen, 32, 136
Southeast Asian workers, 28
Soviet Union, 3, 16, 25
Spanish workers, 19
SPD-FDP coalition, 23
Staatsangehörigkeitsgesetz, 33
Standard German, 3, 51, 57, 140 (n. 6)
Substratum effect: in language, 73; in literature, 128
Sudetenland, 16
Sweden: bilingualism in Finnish children, 75–76

Taufiq, Suleman, 96, 100
Tawada, Yoko, 101
Tekinay, Alev, 100
Third-generation immigrants, 1, 42, 146 (n. 20)
Third Reich, 45–46
Torkan (Iranian writer), 101
Torossi, Eleni, 101
Tschinag, Galsan, 101
Turkish workers, 19, 21, 39, 49, 63, 74–76, 139 (nn. 6, 7)
Turkish writers, 99, 100

Unemployment rates, 44; Baden-Württemberg, 17; North Rhine-Westphalia, 17; Schleswig-Holstein, 17
United States, 3, 76; as immigration country, 12, 83
Üstün, Nevzar, 99

Vereinna(h)mung, 8
Vergangenheitsbewältigung, 46, 136
Vertriebene, 16
Vietnamese workers: in GDR, 28
Volksdeutsche, 30
Vrkljan, Irena, 100

Weimar Republic, 14
Wirtschaftswunder, 16–17
World War I, 13, 14, 20
World War II, 6, 15, 16, 136

Xenolect, 77–81, 142 (n. 20), 143 (n. 23)

Yugoslav workers, 21

www.ingramcontent.com/pod-product-compliance
Lightning Source LLC
Chambersburg PA
CBHW031313150426
43191CB00005B/218